THE RED S
Dive Guide

CW00429335

Text by ALESSANDRO CARLETTI
Photographs by ANDREA GHISOTTI

Editing provided by Diving Science and Technology Corp. (DSAT)
a corporate affiliate of Professional Association of Diving Instructors (PADI)

ABBEVILLE PRESS PUBLISHERS
New York London Paris

THE RED SEA
Dive Guide

CONTENTS

SINAI
ISRAEL

Suez

Eilat
1-2-3 ◦※
Aqaba
4-5-6-7
● 8

● 9

Sharm-
el-Sheikh

EGYPT
● 17
● 18
● 10
●11-12
● 13
19 20-21
└ 14-15-16
● 22-23
● 24
Hurghada
● 25
● 26-27

● 28

Al Quseir
● 29

Port
Berenice
● 30
● 31

● 32
● 33

RED SEA

Jedda ※

● 34
● 35
● 36-37
Port
Sudan
● 38
● 39

SUDAN

SAUDI ARABIA

● 40

Massawa ※
● 41
◦ 42
Al-Hudaydah

ERITREA

YEMEN

GULF OF ADEN

JORDAN

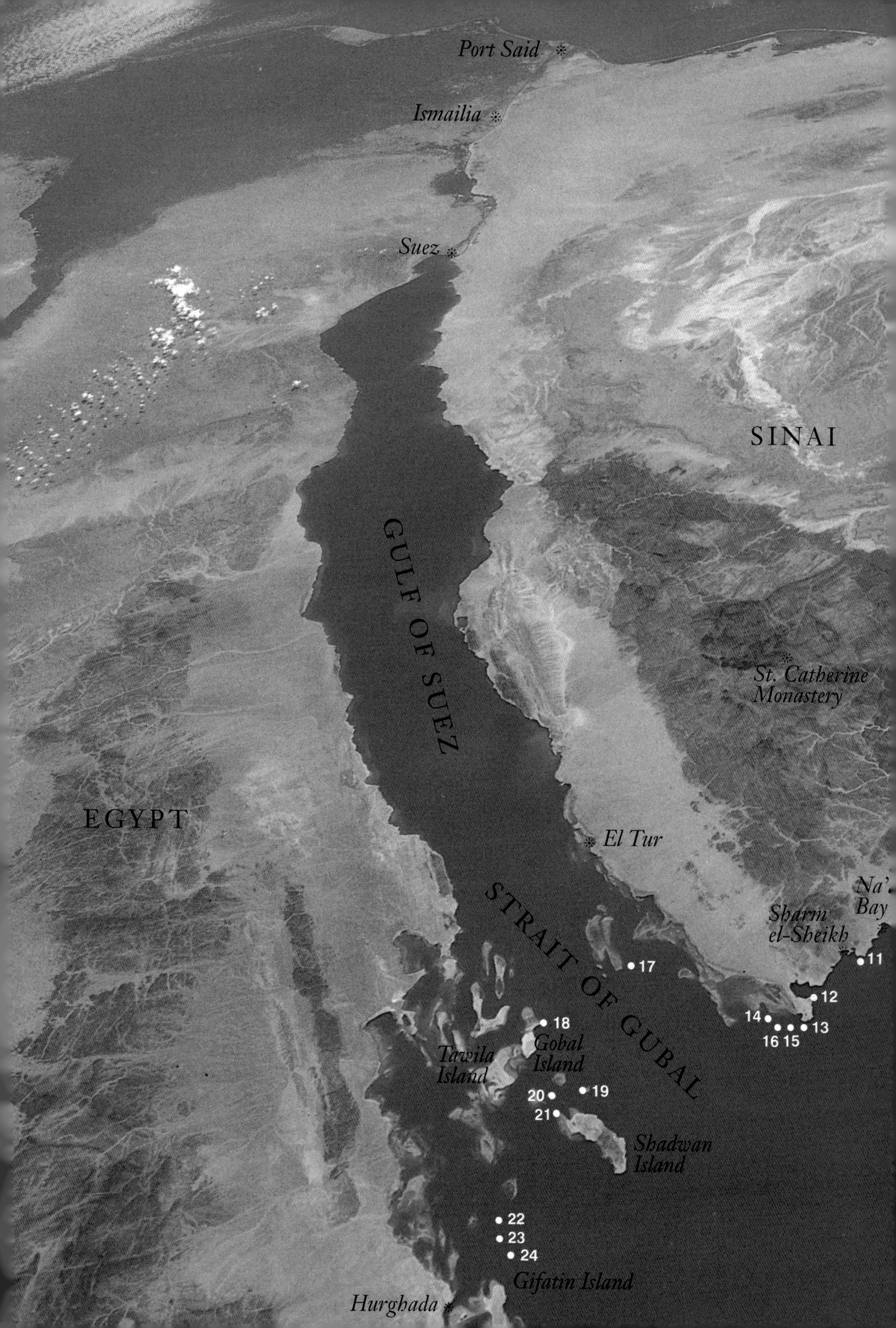

Port Said ✳

Ismailia ✳

Suez ✳

SINAI

GULF OF SUEZ

St. Catherine ✳
Monastery

EGYPT

✳ El Tur

STRAIT OF GUBAL

Na'
Bay

Sharm
el-Sheikh

● 17

● 11

● 12

● 18

14 ● 13
● ● ● ●
16 15

Gobal
Island

Tawila
Island

20 ● ● 19

21 ●

Shadwan
Island

● 22

● 23

● 24

Gifatin Island

Hurghada ✳

ISRAEL

JORDAN

1 - 2 - 3   *Eilat*
4 - 5   *Aqaba*

6 - 7

Nuweiba

8

GULF OF AQABA

Dahab 9

SAUDI
ARABIA

0

*Sanafir
Island*

*Tiran
Island*

RED SEA

INTRODUCTION

European divers have long considered the Red Sea to be a prime dive location, as it is the tropical sea closest to Europe. Divers from around the world now favor it because the Red Sea offers excellent diving both in winter, when other water cool, and in spring and summer, in spite of intense African heat.

After the first adventurous expeditions in the 1950s, often organized with limited resources and great ingenuity, tourism has continually developed in certain areas. Lodging, dive centers, and charter boats specially equipped for underwater cruises are now commonplace. Particularly in recent years, the phenomenon has exploded, and the classic northern sites of Hurghada and Sharm el-Sheikh have become sophisticated and well-equipped world-class dive destinations. The region's political stability and the convenient charter flights linking many European cities directly with these two sites have made this development possible.

The number of divers associated with the tourism boom has naturally posed an environmental threat to the region's reefs and their inhabitants. Fortunately, local authorities created underwater parks, such as Ras Mohammad, at the far southern tip of the Sinai peninsula, with the specific aim of preserving and protecting areas of particular environmental importance. These parks had an immediate and noticeable effect. Today, Ras Mohammad and other dive sites (such as the reefs in the Strait of Tiran, or Careless Reef) are among the finest dives in the world, not just in the Red Sea.

To the south, tourist facilities become less common. The seas here, in spite of regular dive visitors, have a unique aura of mystery, rich in contrasts and unpredictable. Interesting sites are the mythical islet of Zabargad, with its abandoned olivine mines dating to the 16th century B.C.; the small Rocky Island, with its noisy tern population; the Brother Islands, which are little more than crags breaking the surface some hundred miles south of the Sinai coast; and the unsettled waters of Dedalus Reef, which few scuba divers visit.

Still farther south, the Sudan, whose waters are a veritable underwater paradise, seems to close its doors to tourism. Diving here requires determination and adaptability. Lastly, the Dahlak

A

B

C

A. Great fans of gorgonians (Gorgonia ventalina) *open along the walls of the reef, giving the seabed of the northern Red Sea its unmistakable appearance.*
PHOTOGRAPH BY CLAUDIO ZIRALDO

B. Masked butterflyfish (Chaetodon semi-larvatus) *are among the most common and distinctive inhabitants of the coral walls of this sea.*
PHOTOGRAPH BY CLAUDIO ZIRALDO

C. A group of blackspotted grunts (Plectorhynchus gaterinus) *gazes curiously at the photographer.*
PHOTOGRAPH BY VINCENZO PAOLILLO

Islands have been off limits for many years due to the war between Ethiopia and Eritrea.

For a region so important to scuba diving history, it is odd that there has never before been a single book to serve as a complete diver's guide. This book fills that gap and provides serious divers with an overview of the finest dives in the Red Sea, from the far north to the southernmost Dahlak Islands. Each area's entry includes an underwater route map and a 3-dimensional drawing documenting a complete dive.

A Miracle to Be Protected

The Red Sea, home to a fantastic variety of coral and fish, offers an unrivaled diving experience. Separated from the Indian Ocean by the Strait of Suez, the Gulf of Aqaba, and the Strait of Bab el Mandeb, it is a virtually tideless basin with regular currents (northward in winter, southward in summer), and its deep waters are warmed up to 86°F (30°C) by volcanic activity on the seabed. More than 400 species of coral have been recorded so far, and 20 percent of the fish population can be found nowhere else in the world.

Coral's strength lies in its ability to regenerate and live in harmony with the rest of the reef's inhabitants. The Red Sea's reefs, though, are threatened daily by the region's heavy freighter traffic, particularly oil tankers. Everyone—governments and corporations as well as individuals—must do all they can to keep the Red Sea safe from these potential hazards. Careless scuba divers are a hazard, too, so treat the coral reefs with respect; their beauty is fragile. Here are some general guidelines to follow while diving the Red Sea:

- Remove nothing (alive, dead, or fossilized) from the beaches and seabed.
- Do not drive vehicles on the coral waterfront areas.
- Do not litter the beaches or throw anything into the water.
- Do not drop anchor on the reef; use the special moorings provided in protected areas.
- Do not spearfish or sport fish in protected areas.
- Never spearfish while using scuba equipment.
- Do not feed the fish.

E

F

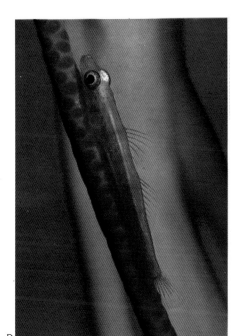

D. A tiny blenny (Helcogramma sp.) poised on a slender branch of coral.
PHOTOGRAPH BY PAOLO FOSSATI

E. Divers explore the wreck of a tugboat that sank off the coast of southern Egypt.
PHOTOGRAPH BY ANDREA GHISOTTI

F. The intricate structure of a branch of soft coral (Dendronephthya sp.).
PHOTOGRAPH BY JEFF ROTMAN

D

- Make sure you do not damage the seabed while diving.
- If you are a beginning diver, limit your diving to areas that cannot be damaged (sandy seabeds with scattered coral formations) until you master buoyancy control.

Lastly, read books and watch films about underwater fauna before you go. The best way to protect the reefs and really enjoy your dive is with information.

A

B

A. A splendid specimen of the humphead wrasse (Cheilinus undulatus) *accompanies a diver through the deep seabeds of Ras Mohammad.*
PHOTOGRAPH BY ITAMAR GRINBERG

B. Soft corals in limitless shades are a spectacular feature of the Red Sea.
PHOTOGRAPH BY VINCENZO PAOLILLO

C. A diver takes in the beauty of the Red Sea's soft corals.
PHOTOGRAPH BY ANDREA AND ANTONELLA FERRARI

Scuba Diving Equipment

The success of a diving expedition depends on preparation. This is especially true of the Red Sea because in Egypt, Sudan, and Eritrea, depending on the type of expedition you choose, access to dive centers may be difficult. Make absolutely sure that you have everything you need, then test it all thoroughly. It is a good idea to have all your equipment professionally serviced at a dive center before your trip. Wet suit choice is extremely important. Even though the Red Sea is warmed by volcanic activity, the entire region is not always warm and tropical. A light $\frac{1}{8}$-in.

(3-mm) wet suit is good year round for the warmer central and southern waters, but the northern waters of Sinai and the Egyptian coast cool to about 75°F (24°C) during the winter, and the underdressed diver can suffer from the cold. A ³/₁₆-in. (5-mm) wet suit with a hood is best from the middle of November to the end of March. For the rest of the year a ¹/₈-in. (3-mm) wet suit is sufficient, but always make sure it covers as much of the body as possible to protect the skin from abrasion by the coral.

The sea floor and the beaches are dotted with sharp pieces of coral, so wear comfortable boots with thick soles and open-heeled fins to accommodate them.

A buoyancy control device, which carries the tank, is essential. It is fundamental to diving in a number of locations in the Red Sea. The system for attaching the jacket to the tank should give solid support to an 80-cubic-foot (12-liter) tank, commonly used in local dive centers. These tanks are usually equipped with standard K-valves and have no reserve mechanism; alternate air source second stages, or a completely redundant backup system, are highly recommended.

Along with mask, fins, and snorkel, bring a good knife, a pair of reef gloves for protection from coral and certain animals, and an underwater flashlight for looking into dark caves and grottoes and for night dives. Always bring your dive tables, watch, spare parts, and a small box of tools. The spare parts should include:

- mask and mask strap
- regulator mouthpiece
- spare o-rings for the tanks
- straps for fins and knife

The tool box should include:

- a tube of neoprene adhesive for wet suit repairs
- hex wrenches to unscrew the outlets of the first-stage regulator (with the spare stoppers)
- appropriate wrenches for hose attachment
- a screwdriver

A Swiss Army knife or a multi-tool available in dive stores is always useful. A dive computer, which calculates nitrogen absorption continuously, is extremely helpful. Dive computers also make it easy to track nitrogen levels during multiple dives over several days.

D

E

F

D. A scuba diver lights up a school of masked butterflyfish.
PHOTOGRAPH BY VINCENZO PAOLILLO

E. A moray eel (Gymnothorax javanicus) *emerges to take a closer look at a diver.*
PHOTOGRAPH BY ANDREA AND ANTONELLA FERRARI

F. The buoyancy compensator is required equipment in many locations.
PHOTOGRAPH BY MARCELLO BERTINETTI

Photographic Equipment

Divers traveling to the Red Sea will definitely want to bring home images of the colorful coral and fish they saw during their dives. A simple amphibious camera capable of withstanding the pressure at 15 or 30 feet (5 or 10 meters) can take decent images, especially with high-speed film, which needs no artificial lighting and can capture a wide range of warm colors.

Better pictures are taken with more sophisticated equipment. The Nikonos camera, one of the few underwater cameras with interchangeable lenses, is used by professionals and serious amateurs. The extremely high-quality wide-angle lenses range from 15 to 20 millimeters. For action shots, the Nikonos is unbeatable, due to its compactness and the simplicity of its viewing and focusing system. It is less impressive with normal and telephoto lenses: a high minimum focus and a very limited depth of field make the user wish for a single lens reflex system.

To take pictures of fish using macro systems, the best choices are a normal dry-land reflex camera with a waterproof housing or the *Nikonos RS* reflex camera. These cameras can focus and frame precisely, and the vast range of lenses allows a choice between macro, telephoto, and wide angle.

The most useful type of film is slide film in the mid- to low-range sensitivity (50–100 ASA/ISO), which is adequate in good light in very clear water or when used with 1 or 2 electronic strobes to obtain color at depth. Strobes also help in the top few meters under the surface, where the eye may distinguish among colors that film shows as more filtered, tending to brown.

For broad environmental shots use the fill-in technique, which is a careful mix of sunlight and artificial light: the foreground full of color from the flash and the background a perfect blue in the filtering sunlight.

Use a light meter to calculate the amount of available light, which can be more intense in the top few meters under the surface, especially over a sandy bottom, than it appears to the eye.

For distant subjects—more than 10 feet (3 to 4 meters) away—use only available light with the right film. Even the clearest water is full of suspended particles that will appear as large bright spots if the photograph is taken with a strobe.

A

B

C

A. The Nikonos is currently the only amphibious camera with interchangeable lenses.
PHOTOGRAPH BY
MARCELLO BERTINETTI

B. A number of reliable waterproof movie camera cases are available.
PHOTOGRAPH BY
ITAMAR GRINBERG

C. A scuba diver photographing the Thistlegorm's *deck.*
PHOTOGRAPH BY ANDREA
AND ANTONELLA FERRARI

Dangerous Fish and Corals

Be aware of poisonous and venomous fish and coral when diving in tropical seas. The Scorpaenidae family of fish is the most notorious: the spines of the lionfish (*Pterois volitans* and *Pterois radiata*) and scorpionfish (*Scorpaenopsis diabolus* and *Scorpaenopsis barbatus*) give extremely painful puncture wounds that cause dangerously high fevers, but the stonefish (*Synanceia verrucosa*) can deliver a lethal sting. All of the 35 known species in this family can inject neurotoxins, resulting in acute pain, local swelling that spreads, hypothermia (extreme cold), tachycardia (fast heartbeat), heavy sweating, then fever. The effects of neurotoxins can be reduced by applying very hot packs to the stung limb. Venomous corals include fire coral (*Millepora dichotoma* or *Millepora complanata*, a distant relative of the jellyfish), whose yellow, white-tipped fans eject a minute stinging thread when touched. If you are stung, wash the area thoroughly with sea water and apply cortisone cream. Nocturnal, and far rarer, are the venomous urchins: *Asthenosoma varium* has long red spines tipped with white venom sacs and *Diadema* has long black spines. Bluespotted stingrays (*Taeniura lymma*) have a venomous tail sting, and a bite from the moray eel (*Gymnothorax* sp.) can easily become infected. Remember, none of these species attack humans unprovoked, and a sting or a bite is easily avoided by paying attention to what you touch when diving and by wearing the proper protective gear (see Scuba Diving Equipment, page 8) in case of an accident.

D. The lionfish does not attack unless provoked, but be aware that its dorsal sting is poisonous.
PHOTOGRAPH BY PAOLO FOSSATI

E. A close-up view of the sharp spines protruding from the base of the surgeonfish's tail.
PHOTOGRAPH BY ANDREA GHISOTTI

F. Scorpaenopsis barbatus has excellent camouflage and poisonous dorsal shafts connected to poison sacs, making it particularly dangerous.
PHOTOGRAPH BY ANDREA AND ANTONELLA FERRARI

G. The bluespotted stingray is usually quite timid, but has two sharp poisonous spines at the tip of its tail.
PHOTOGRAPH BY ANDREA AND ANTONELLA FERRARI

H. The poison secreted from the dorsal sting of the stonefish is extremely toxic and can kill humans.
PHOTOGRAPH BY GIANFRANCO D'AMATO

A. The city of Eilat, on the shore of the Gulf of Aqaba, is at the southernmost point of Israel, on the Jordanian and Egyptian border. Equipped with impressive tourist facilities, each year it receives some 1 million visitors, especially scuba divers and naturalists.
PHOTOGRAPH BY
MARCELLO BERTINETTI

B. The submarine Jacqueline *setting out on an excursion from Coral Beach Underwater Observatory in Eilat.*
PHOTOGRAPH BY
ITAMAR GRINBERG

C. Even those who do not scuba dive can experience the thrill of the teeming underwater world aboard the Jacqueline, *which descends to almost 200 feet (60 meters).*
PHOTOGRAPH BY
ITAMAR GRINBERG

Eilat is the southernmost city of Israel, a thriving vacation spot with fine hotels that is easily accessed by air. It is situated at the tip of the Gulf of Aqaba and lies within the global desert belt, which makes for sparse land vegetation but amazingly lush marine flora and fauna.

The shores and coral reefs of Eilat, from the Jordanian border in the north to the Egyptian border in the south, are protected by the Nature Reserve Authority; most of the area is open beach, but Coral Beach, the northernmost coral reef in the world and about a mile of the richest reef in the area, is a private nature reserve with paid admission.

The waters of the Gulf of Aqaba are clear, bright, and warm. Its shores are lined with many strip reefs 30 to 45 feet (10 to 15 meters) from the high tide mark, creating a shallow lagoon between the reef and the shore and offering a magical underwater world.

Most of the Red Sea's coral reefs grow on granite, and their colorful walls plunge sheer into the sea's depths, hidden to all but divers. In 1975, Coral World Underwater Observatory was built to allow everyone to view the reefs. The observatory is a metal tower set directly above and 20 feet (6 meters) into the reef, attached to the shore by a walkway. Twenty-one underwater windows face seabeds filled with tropical fish and coral. At the top of the tower, 75 feet (23 meters) above sea level, the

A

B

C

D. A pier 325 feet (100 meters) long leads to the circular steel structure of the observatory, which rises 75 feet (23 meters) above the surface of the sea. From the top it is possible to see the 4 nations that verge on the bay of Eilat: Israel, Jordan, Saudi Arabia, and Egypt.
PHOTOGRAPH BY
MARCELLO BERTINETTI

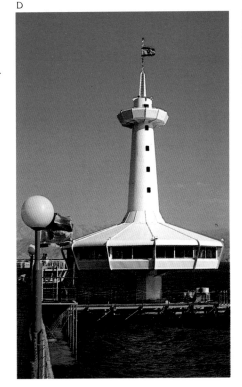

E. The circular structure of the tower offers 21 windows looking out onto the seabed.
PHOTOGRAPH BY
CESARE GEROLIMETTO

F. The aquariums of Coral World house all the main species of fish found in the Red Sea.
PHOTOGRAPH BY
CESARE GEROLIMETTO

G. At Dolphin Reef you can swim with large rays, who have become accustomed to the presence of humans and can be petted.
PHOTOGRAPH BY
ITAMAR GRINBERG

H. Although fed by humans, the dolphins have not lost their natural instinct to hunt.
PHOTOGRAPH BY
ITAMAR GRINBERG

I. Divers can approach the dolphins under the supervision of a guide.
PHOTOGRAPH BY
ITAMAR GRINBERG

A. The seabeds of Eilat owe their remarkable wealth of fish and hard and soft corals to the unvarying water temperature.
PHOTOGRAPH BY
ITAMAR GRINBERG

B. A group of masked butterflyfish (Chaetodon semilarvatus) *swims in close formation just off the wall of the reef.*
PHOTOGRAPH BY
VINCENZO PAOLILLO

C. Two butterflyfish (Chaetodon fasciatus) *swim just under the surface.*
PHOTOGRAPH BY
ANDREA GHISOTTI

A

B

C

D. A twobar anemonefish (Amphiprion bicinctus) *hides among the tentacles of a sea anemone, its customary refuge; these tentacles are toxic to all other species of fish.*
PHOTOGRAPH BY
ITAMAR GRINBERG

E. A coral grouper (Cephalopholis miniata) *climbs up the wall of the reef.*
PHOTOGRAPH BY
MARCELLO BERTINETTI

F. The valves of a giant clam (Tridacna maxima) *gape from out of the delicate formations of soft corals.*
PHOTOGRAPH BY
ITAMAR GRINBERG

deserts of Egypt, Israel, Jordan, and Saudi Arabia can be seen beyond the water.

Many species of fish, corals, and other life forms, usually seen only by scuba divers at great depths, can be seen in Coral World's aquariums, which include a shark tank and a turtle tank. Coral World also offers an introductory dive (even for the novice) and a trip 200 feet (60 meters) beneath the surface on an hour-long submarine ride aboard the *Jacqueline*.

D

E

F

Japanese Gardens

BY HANAN GOLOMBEK

Named for its table corals shaped like pagodas, this reef is one of the most magnificent of its kind. It stretches almost 1,000 feet (300 meters) north from Coral World at depths of 40 to 150 feet (12 to 47 meters). To reach the reef, enter at the southern gate of Coral Beach (ticket required), where there is space to park and change. Call the beach in advance to reserve dive time; only 20 divers are allowed per day. Buoys clearly mark dive entry and route. Visitors can either dive down and northward along the wall of the reef, rising with the seabed, or cruise northward in shallow water—no more than 40 feet (12 meters)—and back again by the reef wall. Decompression stops can be made on the return journey. Divers may see (and should be careful of) the submarine *Jacqueline* and some glass-bottomed boats.

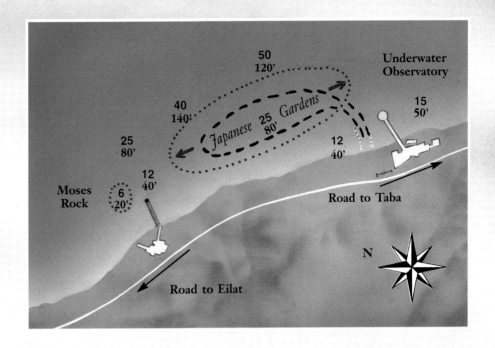

Underwater
Observatory

50
120'

40
140'

25
80'

Japanese 25 *Gardens*
80'

15
50'

12
40'

12
40'

6
20'

Moses
Rock

Road to Taba

N

Road to Eilat

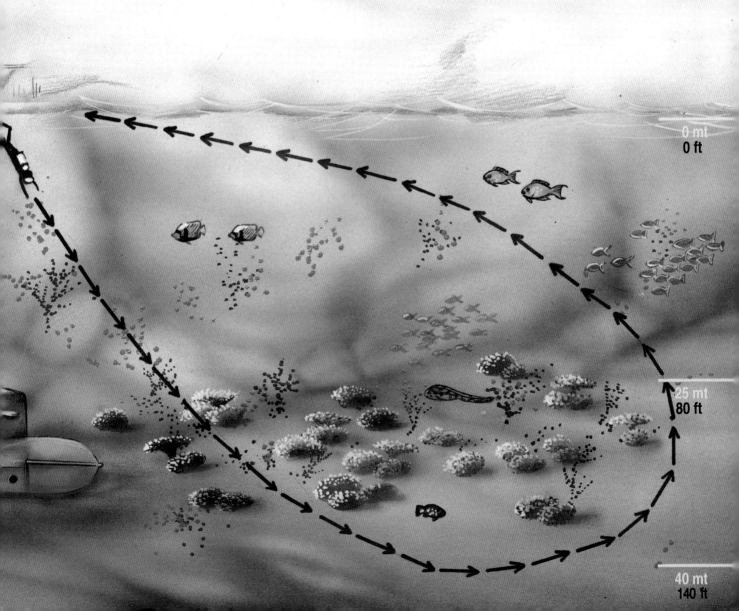

0 mt
0 ft

25 mt
80 ft

40 mt
140 ft

Moses Rock

BY HANAN GOLOMBEK

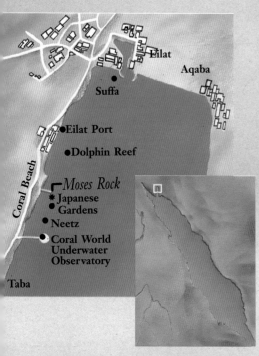

The half mile (700 meters) between the entrance to Coral Beach and the Underwater Observatory is Eilat's most beautiful area—the richest in corals and fish. To enjoy these waters, either swim out over the reef's flat top and along a route marked by buoys, or use the bridge that ends just west of Moses Rock, a beautiful column of coral in 26 feet (8 meters) of water that reaches almost to the surface. Its corals are very brightly colored, and many species of fish live around it, unafraid of divers. The surrounding seabed is sandy with many coral colonies, and slopes to a depth of 155 feet (47 meters).

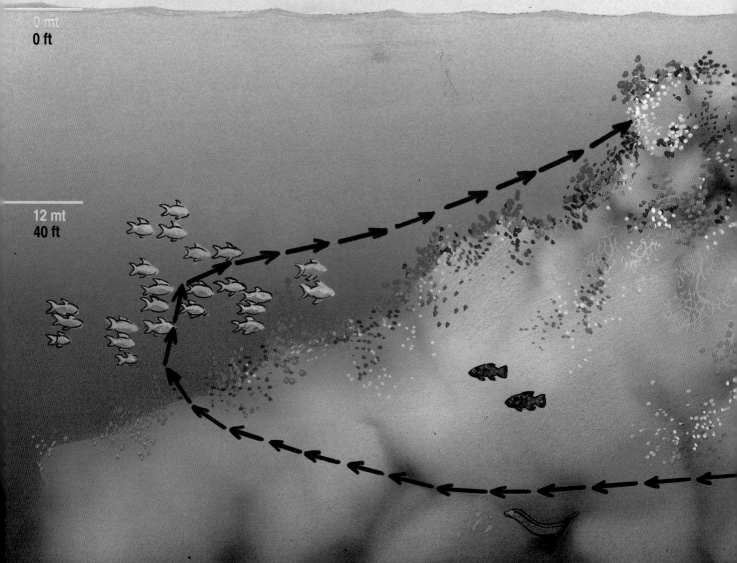

0 mt
0 ft

12 mt
40 ft

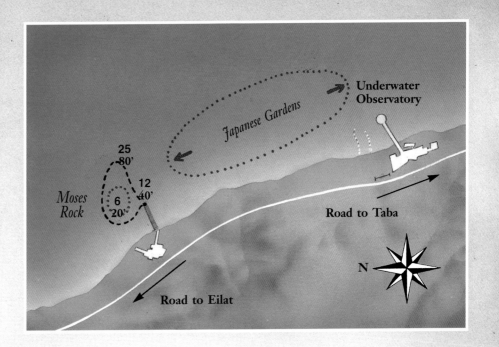

Moses
Rock

25
80'

6
20'

12
40'

Japanese Gardens

Underwater
Observatory

Road to Taba

Road to Eilat

N

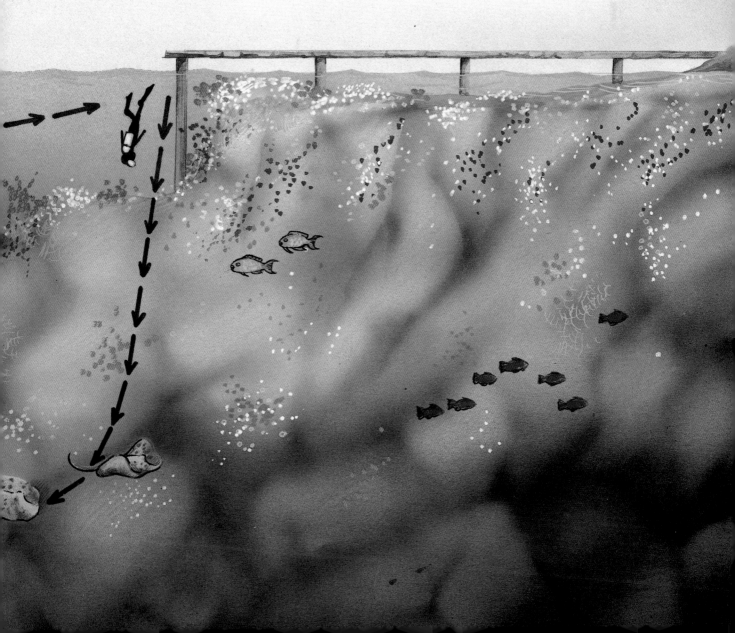

Dolphin Reef, Eilat

BY HANAN GOLOMBEK

The dolphins who live on this reef are very friendly to humans and love to swim with scuba divers—they begin to approach as soon as you enter the water. But remember, although they are fenced in and living in captivity, they are the masters of this environment. To dive with them in their natural habitat is a special privilege. Everyone who dives off Dolphin Reef must be accompanied by a

Eilat

Aqaba

Suffa

Eilat Port

Dolphin Reef

Coral Beach

Moses Rock
Japanese
Gardens
Neetz
Coral World
Underwater
Observatory

Taba

0 mt
0 ft

3 mt
10 ft

8 mt
25 ft

15 mt
50 ft

specially trained guide. The guides are old friends of the dolphins, but visiting divers must follow the rules. Most important, never grab at them as they swim by.

This sea floor enclosure covers 6 square miles (10,000 square meters) and goes 60 feet (18 meters) deep. In it you can get close to large rays, and explore a small wreck, called the *Dan*, at 19 to 30 feet (6 to 10 meters).

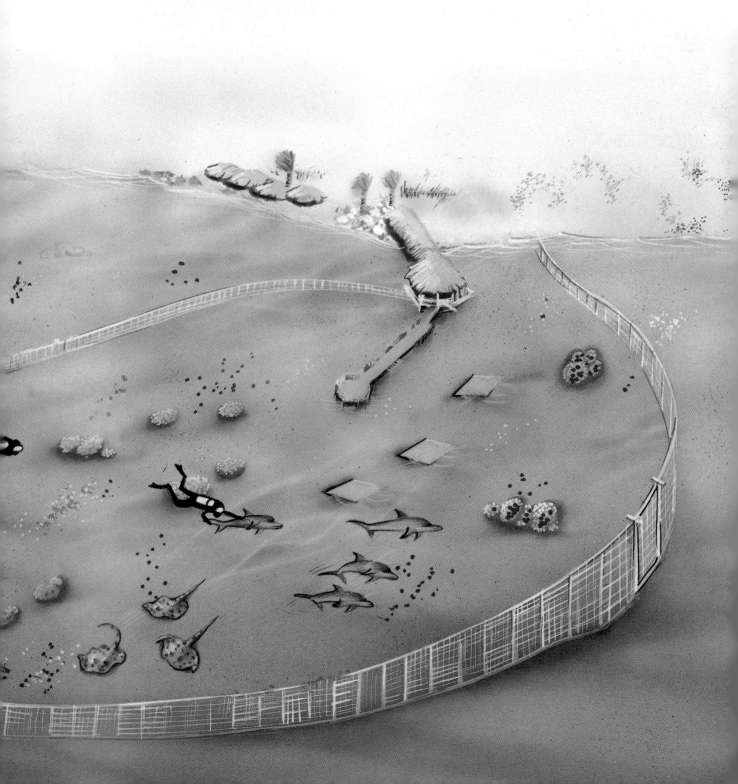

The Suffa Wreck

BY GIL BUNIM

A missile-launching corvette, about 150 feet (45 meters) long, lies 200 feet (66 meters) from the coast of Eilat, at a depth of 65 feet (20 meters). This ship and 3 others like it were built in France for the Israeli navy. It was still in Cherbourg port when the French declared an embargo on hostile Middle Eastern nations during the Yom Kippur War in 1973, but was smuggled out by sailors. It was one of the first warships to pass through the Strait of Suez following the declaration of peace between Egypt and Israel in 1979, and it served in the Mediterranean until 1990. When the *Suffa* lost its military usefulness, the Israeli Scuba Diving Federation dismantled it and sent it to the bottom to create an interesting dive site.

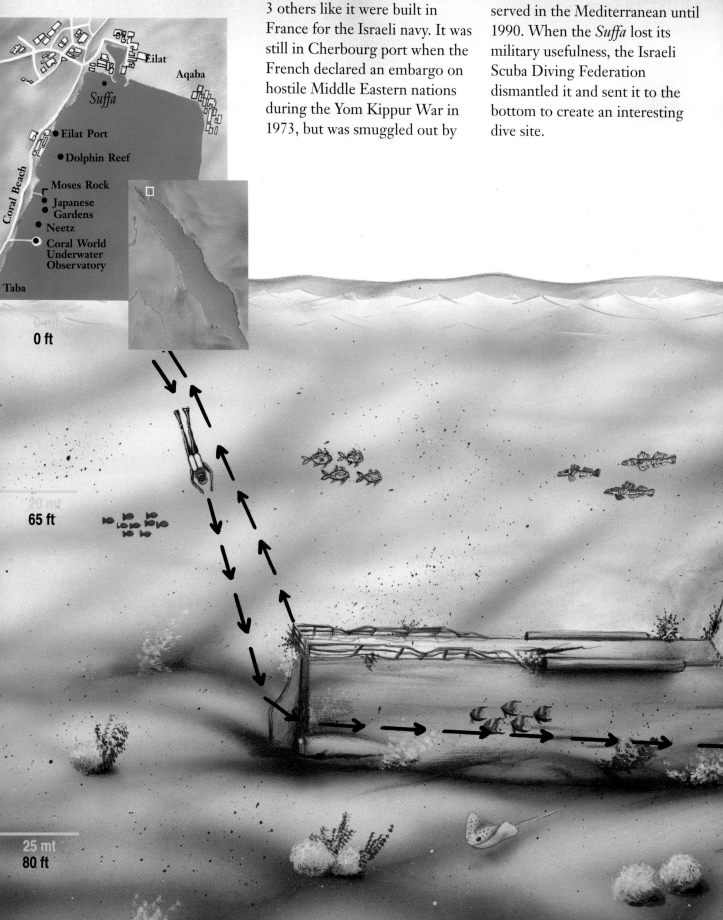

Eilat

Aqaba

Suffa

Eilat Port

Dolphin Reef

Coral Beach

Moses Rock

Japanese Gardens

Neetz

Coral World Underwater Observatory

Taba

0 ft

65 ft

20 mt

25 mt

80 ft

Now being colonized by the fauna of the Red Sea, the *Suffa* "wreck" makes a remarkable dive from the beach, following the sandy seabed, which drops gently to depths of 65 to 82 feet (20 to 25 meters).

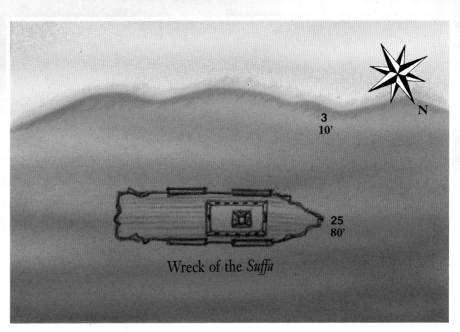

3
10'

25
80'

Wreck of the *Suffa*

The Neetz Wreck

BY GIL BUNIM

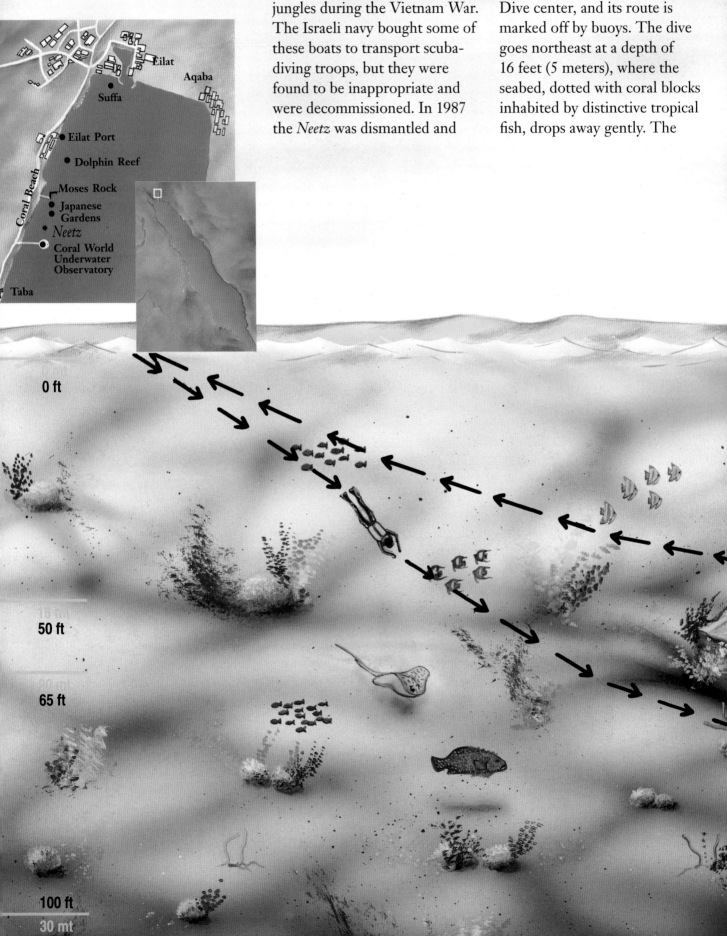

The *Neetz*, a small fighting craft, 50 feet (15 meters) long and 16.5 feet (5 meters) wide, was designed by the U.S. Army and used to navigate rivers and jungles during the Vietnam War. The Israeli navy bought some of these boats to transport scuba-diving troops, but they were found to be inappropriate and were decommissioned. In 1987 the *Neetz* was dismantled and sent to the bottom just south of the Japanese Gardens to make a dive site for tourists.

This fairly simple dive begins from the beach of the Aqua Sport Dive center, and its route is marked off by buoys. The dive goes northeast at a depth of 16 feet (5 meters), where the seabed, dotted with coral blocks inhabited by distinctive tropical fish, drops away gently. The

Eilat

Aqaba

Suffa

Eilat Port

Dolphin Reef

Moses Rock

Japanese Gardens

Neetz

Coral World Underwater Observatory

Coral Beach

Taba

0 ft

50 ft

65 ft

100 ft

30 mt

Neetz, now encrusted with multi-colored corals and alcyonarians, is found at 79 feet (24 meters). Expert divers can tour the interior, passing through the open compartments. Be prepared to deal with fairly powerful local currents, and with small boats and windsurfers at the surface outside the marked area.

Wreck of the *Neetz*

30
100'

JORDAN
Aqaba

The Hashemite Kingdom of Jordan, to the east of Israel, consists mainly of 37,737 square miles (97,740 square kilometers) of highland plain that slopes gently southward to Saudi Arabia. A deep rift runs through it, with the river Jordan in the north and the Red Sea in the center. The landscape is unique: the Dead Sea, on the border of Israel and Jordan, occupies one of the deepest depressions on the planet. Jordan's capital city, Amman, located in

A. A panoramic view of the city and the harbor of Aqaba, surrounded by desert highlands.
PHOTOGRAPH BY VINCENZO PAOLILLO

B. The fortress of Aqaba was built at the order of the Egyptian sultan el-Ghoury in the 16th century, to protect Muslim pilgrims heading for Mecca. All that survives today are a few ruins of the once imposing structure, built on a square plan, with 4 corner towers.
PHOTOGRAPH BY ANTONIO ATTINI/ WHITE STAR

C. A twobar anemonefish (Amphiprion bicinctus) *swims among the tentacles of a sea anemone.*
PHOTOGRAPH BY MARCO BOSCO

D. A vast array of fish and corals typical of the Red Sea live in the waters off Aqaba. A lovely lionfish (Pterois volitans) *is in the foreground.*
PHOTOGRAPH BY ROBERTO RINALDI

E. A superb branch of a pink alcyonarian embellishes the metal structures of the Cedar Pride *wreck.*
PHOTOGRAPH BY VINCENZO PAOLILLO

the center of the country, has all the characteristics of a modern European city yet retains evidence (including many Roman ruins) of its rich history.

Aqaba, Jordan's outlet into the Red Sea's underwater paradise, is a small, modern city located 240 miles (385 kilometers) south of Amman; Eilat is only 1 mile (2 kilometers) and a border away from Aqaba, and the border is increasingly easy to cross. Particularly colorful fish and

coral live in the seabeds off Aqaba, and visitors to the Red Sea have become the city's main concern; plenty of water sports are offered in addition to scuba diving.

Away from the water you can enjoy the Byzantine cathedral of the Pink City, or a horse ride in the interior. Consider taking a trip to the spectacular desert landscape of Wadi Rum, to watch the sun set and enjoy local cuisine and music in an Arab tent. Jordan's desert conceals the ruins

F. A scuba diver illuminates a number of splendid alcyonarians.
PHOTOGRAPH BY ROBERTO RINALDI

G. A pair of Red Sea bannerfish (Heniochus diphreutes) *swim in the shelter of the reef.*
PHOTOGRAPH BY CLAUDIO ZIRALDO

H. Multicolored corals, alcyonarians, and gorgonians, with a coral umbrella reaching to the surface, create an unrivaled seascape.
PHOTOGRAPH BY ROBERTO RINALDI

of many lost civilizations, among them Petra, an ancient cliff city 110 miles (175 kilometers) north of Aqaba. Petra is a huge, architecturally beautiful complex, set in volcanic hills among rocks of remarkable color and structure. Jordan is a wonderful place to take in both the lush underwater world and some of the best desert attractions of the Red Sea region.

The Cedar Pride *Wreck*

BY OSAMA ROSHDY

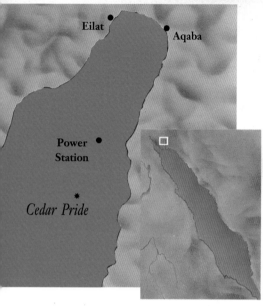

The freighter that lies on the seabed of Aqaba, registered with Lloyd's of London and flying a Greek flag, was originally called the *San Bruno*. It was purchased by a Lebanese company in 1982, renamed *Cedar Pride*, and anchored in Aqaba harbor. There it caught fire and was badly damaged. A year later, the owners decided to present it to the prince of Jordan, who donated it to the

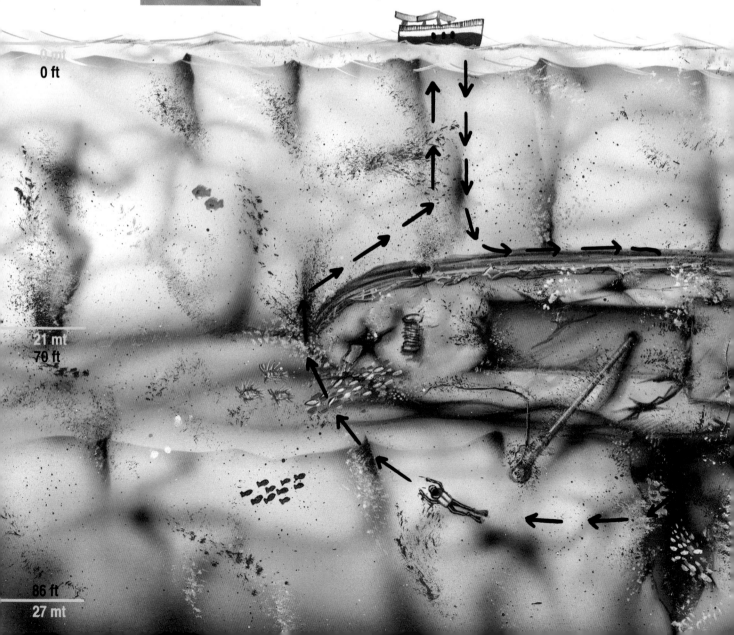

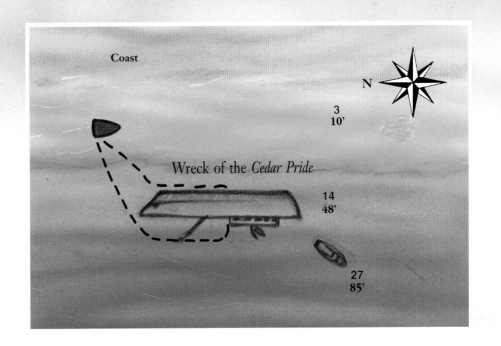

Coast

N

3
10'

Wreck of the *Cedar Pride*

14
48'

27
85'

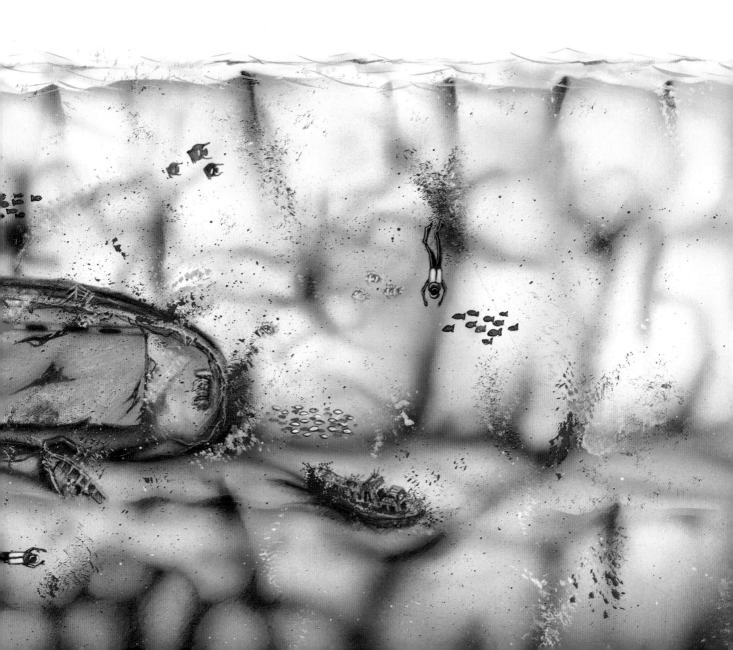

A

C

D

B

*A. The skeletal re-
mains of a dinghy from
the* Cedar Pride *are
evidence of the violent
explosion that sent the
ship to the bottom.*
PHOTOGRAPH BY
VINCENZO PAOLILLO

B. The Cedar Pride,
*completely covered with
multicolored alcyonar-
ians, makes for spectac-
ular photographs.*
PHOTOGRAPH BY
VINCENZO PAOLILLO

scuba-diving community in
Aqaba. It was moved some distance south and was sent to the
bottom, 330 feet (100 meters)
from the coast, with a charge of
dynamite. Now perched on the
summit of the reef with its dinghy
dangling from its side, only 30 to
90 feet (9 to 27 meters) underwater, the wreck can be explored
even by beginning divers.

There are 2 possible ap-
proaches to the wreck: from the
beach by following the downward
slope of the reef, or directly from
above by using one of the local
dive centers' boats. A deep fissure

*C, D. The wreck of
a small fishing boat
not far from the*
Cedar Pride.
PHOTOGRAPHS BY
VINCENZO PAOLILLO

E. The screw of the Cedar Pride, *heavily encrusted, extends into the endless blue waters.*
PHOTOGRAPH BY
VINCENZO PAOLILLO

F. All the surfaces of the Cedar Pride *are now inhabited by countless fish and corals.*
PHOTOGRAPH BY
VINCENZO PAOLILLO

in the reef at the side of the wreck permits a thorough exploration. Remarkably big and colorful alcyonarians cover the wreck, and brightly colored coral fish throng around it. You may spot a solitary humphead wrasse or a sea turtle; about 130 feet (40 meters) west of the wreck, a crocodile fish has claimed a small boat as its home.

E

F

G. Thanks to the remarkable fertility and clarity of the waters of the Red Sea, soft corals can grow on every kind of surface, including the hull of the Cedar Pride.
PHOTOGRAPH BY
VINCENZO PAOLILLO

H. A solitary humphead wrasse (Cheilinus undulatus) *wends its way through a forest of alcyonarians.*
PHOTOGRAPH BY
ROBERTO RINALDI

G

H

Power Station

BY OSAMA ROSHDY

ower Station offers one of Aqaba's most exciting dives to divers at all levels of expertise. The reef wall is sheer to 16.5 feet (5 meters), gently slopes to 46 feet (14 meters), and then drops away steeply to 150 feet (40 meters). The best way to start the dive is from a boat anchored 150 feet (40 meters) from shore; descend to 46 feet (14 meters) and move southward. At 56 feet (16 meters) there is a coral pinnacle, home to a frogfish (*Antennarius coccineus*) and many brightly colored coral fish. Continue to the recommended depth of 82 feet (25 meters) and head north along the coral wall; you will see large groupers (*Epinephelus* sp.), pufferfish (*Arothon* sp.), frogfish, and numerous varieties of coral. To return to the boat, head for shallower waters, southward to the descent line.

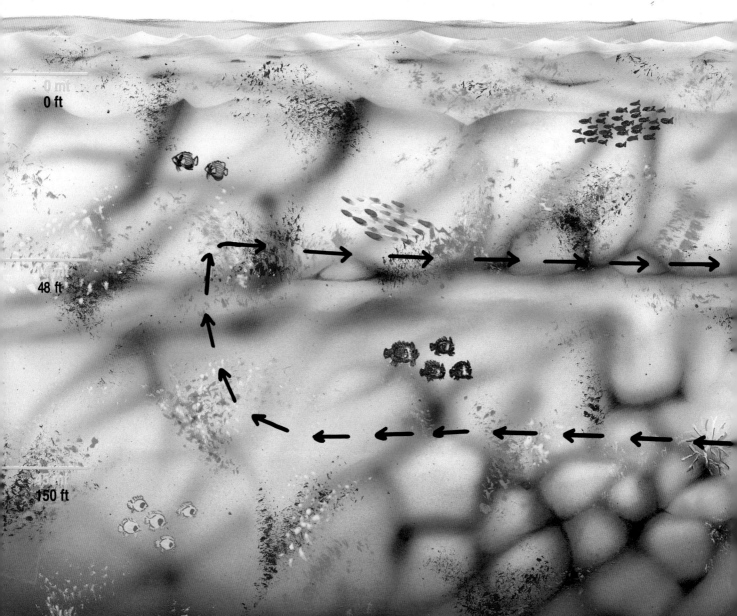

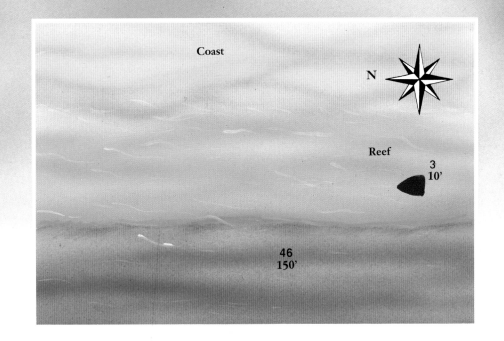

NORTHERN EGYPT
Sharm el-Sheikh

Sharm el-Sheikh, once just a small fishing village, is now a major tourist facility on the east coast of the Sinai desert. The climate is cool in winter—68°F (20°C)—and hot and muggy in summer—104°F (40°C). Sheltered by desert highlands from the powerful north wind, which can interfere with diving in the Red Sea, its beautiful waters are unfailingly warm and inviting; a Lycra suit is sufficient in summer. Sharm caters specifically to tourists, with banks, post offices, car and motorcycle rentals, horse riding, trips into the Sinai desert, and especially scuba diving. Each hotel has its own dive center, offering daily boat excursions with 2 guided dives, night dives, instruction, and equipment rentals. Underwater cruises from Sharm visit all the finest dive sites along the west coast of Sinai.

Sharm was the first basin in the Red Sea to be protected by environmental laws. The National Park of Ras Mohammad, established in 1989, hires a permanent staff of scientists and rangers to enforce these laws and research the area's wildlife and geology. Because of this, the beauty of the coast and waters has remained intact in spite of heavy tourism.

A. The Gulf of Sharm el-Sheikh opens out into the Red Sea at the end of the Sinai desert.
PHOTOGRAPH BY
ITAMAR GRINBERG

B. Na'ama Bay, near Sharm el-Sheikh, is a favorite destination for European tourists.
PHOTOGRAPH BY
ITAMAR GRINBERG

C. The desert reaches the edge of the sea along the coast around Na'ama.
PHOTOGRAPH BY
MARCELLO BERTINETTI

D. The cape of Ras Mohammad is one of the most famous dive sites in the Red Sea.
PHOTOGRAPH BY
MARCELLO BERTINETTI

E

Na'ama Bay, just north of the original fishing village, is the hub of Sharm el-Sheikh. Some of the cosmopolitan hotels along the beach date back to the Israeli occupation of the Sinai—the Hilton Fayrouz, the Möwenpick, the Ghazala, and the Aquamarine. Sheikh Coast is a new resort with a hotel, individual cottages, and beachside apartments, located just north of Na'ama Bay.

There are direct flights to Sharm from many cities, especially in Europe. Make sure that your visa for Egypt applies to the entire country, not just Sharm, or you will miss out on trips beyond the cape of Ras Mohammad.

E. The lushness of the reef and the phenomenal depths of the sea at Ras Mohammad provide sensational dives.
PHOTOGRAPH BY ANDREA AND ANTONELLA FERRARI

F. The great fans of gorgonians extending their branches toward the open sea are one of the most distinctive features of Ras Mohammad.
PHOTOGRAPH BY VINCENZO PAOLILLO

G. A reef wall densely covered with multicolored soft corals.
PHOTOGRAPH BY VINCENZO PAOLILLO

H. A number of the most common species of fish found in the seabeds of North Egypt: sweetlips, parrotfish, onespot snappers, and squirrelfish.
PHOTOGRAPH BY GIANFRANCO D'AMATO

F

G

H

NORTHERN EGYPT
Hurghada

Hurghada is about halfway down the Egyptian coast of the Red Sea, 370 miles (600 kilometers) south of Cairo. It is quite cool in winter; you should bring a light jacket in December and January. It is very hot in summer—104°F (40°C)—but there is always a breeze. For a small town, Hurghada has all necessary tourist facilities: banks,

A. Hurghada, once called Ghardaga, was founded by the English in 1909. Today, Hurghada is a major and well-equipped tourist center, and the starting point for many splendid diving expeditions.
PHOTOGRAPH BY
VINCENZO PAOLILLO

post offices, restaurants, stores, and taxis. Hurghada's location is ideal for taking boat trips to the Gobal Islands and the famous reefs of Sha'ab Abu Nuhâs and the Brother Islands, and you can take a bus to Luxor or a plane to Aswan.

In the 1950s, this small fishing village was the scientific research base of Eugenie Clark, who made important contributions to our understanding of the sea in general and the Red Sea in particular.

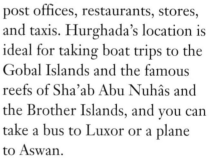

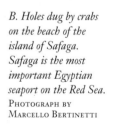

B. Holes dug by crabs on the beach of the island of Safaga. Safaga is the most important Egyptian seaport on the Red Sea.
PHOTOGRAPH BY
MARCELLO BERTINETTI

C. Bright orange scalefin anthias (Anthias squamipinnis) are among the most common inhabitants of the lush coral walls.
PHOTOGRAPH BY
MARCELLO BERTINETTI

E

Mass tourism came to Hurghada in the 1970s and 1980s under President Sadat, whose administration constructed many hotels and tourist villages. Now the southern coast of the village is lined with settlements, including Giftun Village, Sonesta, Princess Village, and Jasmine Village. Each hotel has a fully equipped

D. Shadwan, the largest island in the Red Sea off the Egyptian coast, is identified by a lighthouse that indicates the beginning of the Strait of Gobal channel, which leads to the Suez Canal.
PHOTOGRAPH BY
MARCELLO BERTINETTI

G

F

dive center that offers daily excursions to the archipelago of Hurghada: the 2 islands of Gifatin, the island of Abu Ramada, Magawish, Umm Gamar, Abu Mingar, Abu Hashish, and a number of reefs just breaking the surface.

Despite heavy tourism and the lack of environmental protection, the seabeds are stunning. The variety of coral and quantity of tiny fish that live there permanently are among the greatest to be found along the Egyptian coast, and along deep walls you can see passing pelagic fish.

E. A school of surgeonfish (Naso hexacanthus), *a constant presence on the seabeds of the Brother Islands, passes behind a curtain of large gorgonian fans.*
PHOTOGRAPH BY
ITAMAR GRINBERG

F. A splendid branch of soft coral stands out clearly against the dark blue background of the sea.
PHOTOGRAPH BY
VINCENZO PAOLILLO

G. A number of shortnose blacktail sharks (Carcharhinus wheeleri) *swim the waters around the reef. This particular species can grow up to 6.5 feet (2 meters) and is identified by the black coloring on the rear portion of the tail fin.*
PHOTOGRAPH BY
JACK JACKSON

Nuweiba: The Pipeline

BY LINDA CHAPPEL

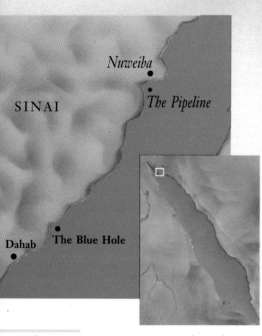

Nuweiba, a magical Bedouin city, has a variety of unspoiled sites for unforgettable dives. Approximately .5 mile (1 kilometer) north of Nuweiba's port is Pipeline Reef, where an incredible multitude of coral fish live. The reef begins at a depth of 3 feet (1 meter) and drops away gently to a depth of 110 feet (33 meters). Its surface area is large—330 by 660 feet (100 by 200 meters)—and many different seaweeds grow on the surrounding sandy seabed.

Pipeline Reef is distinguished by a peculiar series of rounded coral blocks, which resemble little dunes covered with colorful alcyonarians. Only 200 feet (60 meters) from shore, the reef is reached easily from the beach —a great site for beginning divers, who can confidently explore the dune configuration at 26 feet (8 meters).

Experienced divers can enter the water from a boat, not far from an old navigational buoy. By following the chain of the

buoy, they can descend directly to 110 feet (33 meters) and swim back up toward the dunes. All the most distinctive life forms of the Red Sea are here to enjoy— spotted eagle rays *(Aetobatus narinari)*, bluespotted stingrays *(Taeniura lymma)*, sea turtles *(Eretmochelys imbricata)*, moray eels *(Gymnothorax sp.)*, mullets or yellowsaddle goatfish *(Parupeneus cyclostomus)*, parrotfish *(Scarus sp.)*, and spotted unicornfish *(Naso brevirostris)*. At 92 feet (28 meters) there is a superb sea fan.

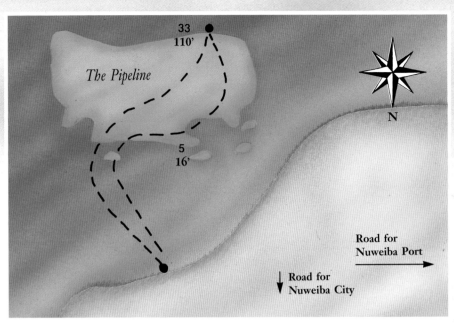

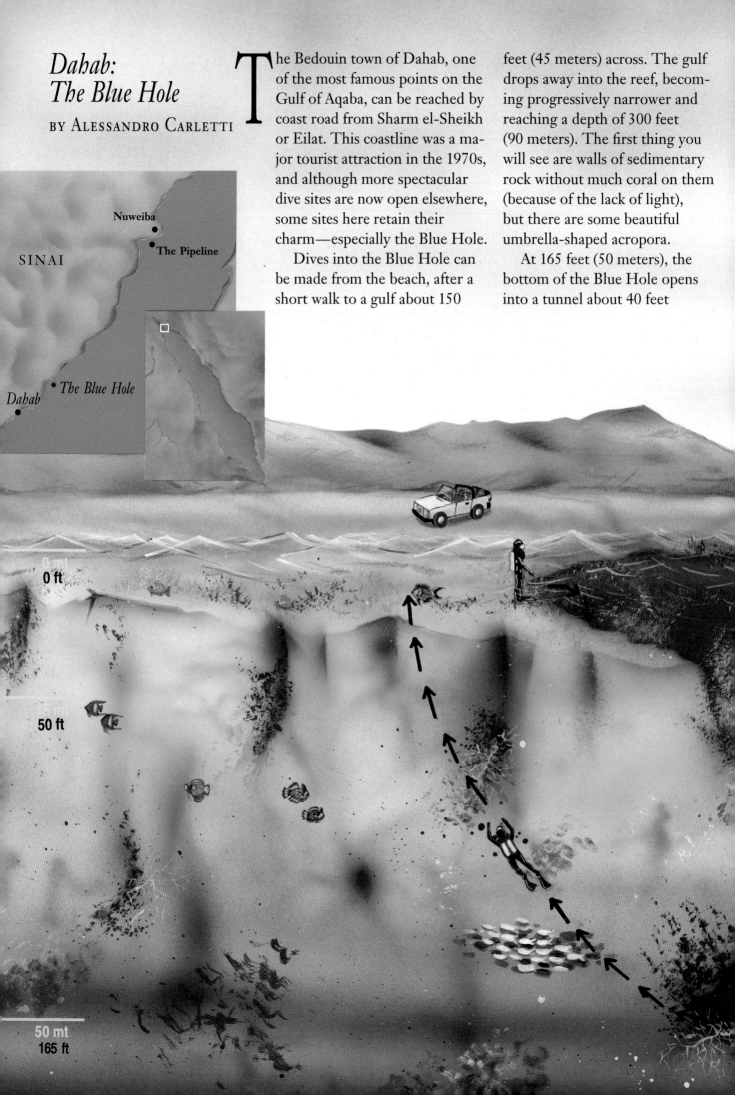

Dahab: The Blue Hole

BY ALESSANDRO CARLETTI

The Bedouin town of Dahab, one of the most famous points on the Gulf of Aqaba, can be reached by coast road from Sharm el-Sheikh or Eilat. This coastline was a major tourist attraction in the 1970s, and although more spectacular dive sites are now open elsewhere, some sites here retain their charm—especially the Blue Hole.

Dives into the Blue Hole can be made from the beach, after a short walk to a gulf about 150 feet (45 meters) across. The gulf drops away into the reef, becoming progressively narrower and reaching a depth of 300 feet (90 meters). The first thing you will see are walls of sedimentary rock without much coral on them (because of the lack of light), but there are some beautiful umbrella-shaped acropora.

At 165 feet (50 meters), the bottom of the Blue Hole opens into a tunnel about 40 feet

SINAI

Nuweiba

The Pipeline

Dahab

* The Blue Hole

0 ft

50 ft

50 mt

165 ft

(12 meters) long that leads out to sea. A spectacular band of blue light penetrates into the tunnel from the sea (hence the name). A wall at the exit of the tunnel, exposed to strong currents, is covered with colorful alcyonarians and sea fans that thrive on the continual passage of water.

This is a deep, challenging dive, not suited to beginners or those uncertain of their abilities.

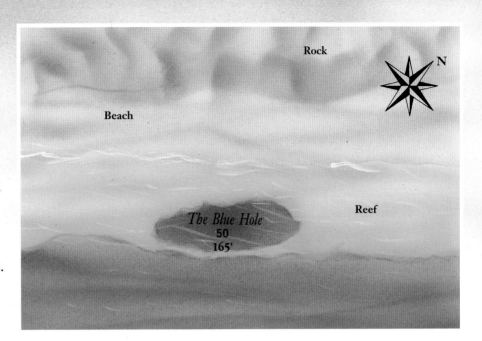

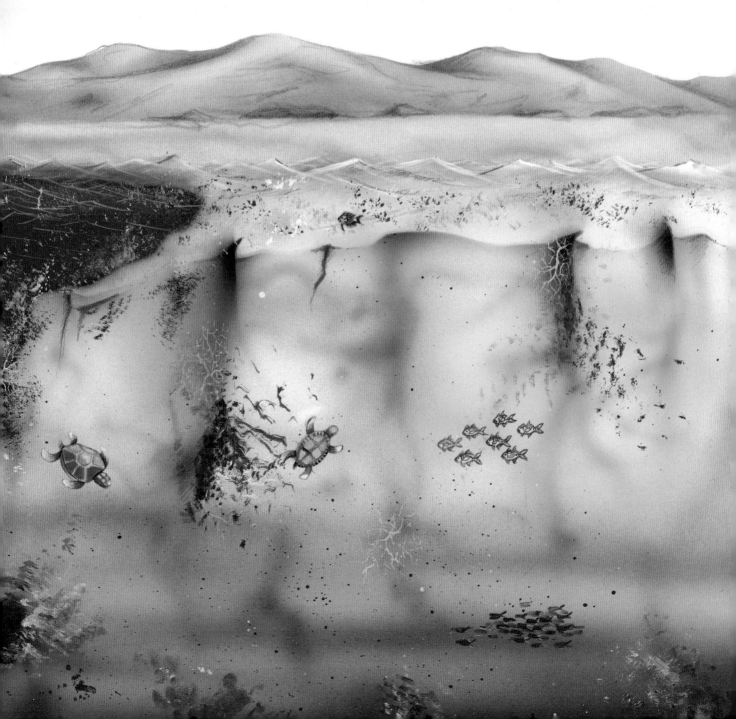

The Strait of Tiran

The Strait of Tiran closes the Gulf of Aqaba twelve miles northeast of Sharm el-Sheikh. The area lies on the gigantic tectonic fault that begins under the Dead Sea, continues along the valley of the Jordan River and a great part of the Red Sea, and ends in the region of the great African Lakes. This is why the Gulf of Aqaba, barely 5.5 miles (9 kilometers) at its widest, is over half a mile (1,000 meters) deep at its center, and the Strait of Tiran over 820 feet (250 meters) deep.

Four reefs (actually the pinnacles of a single underwater

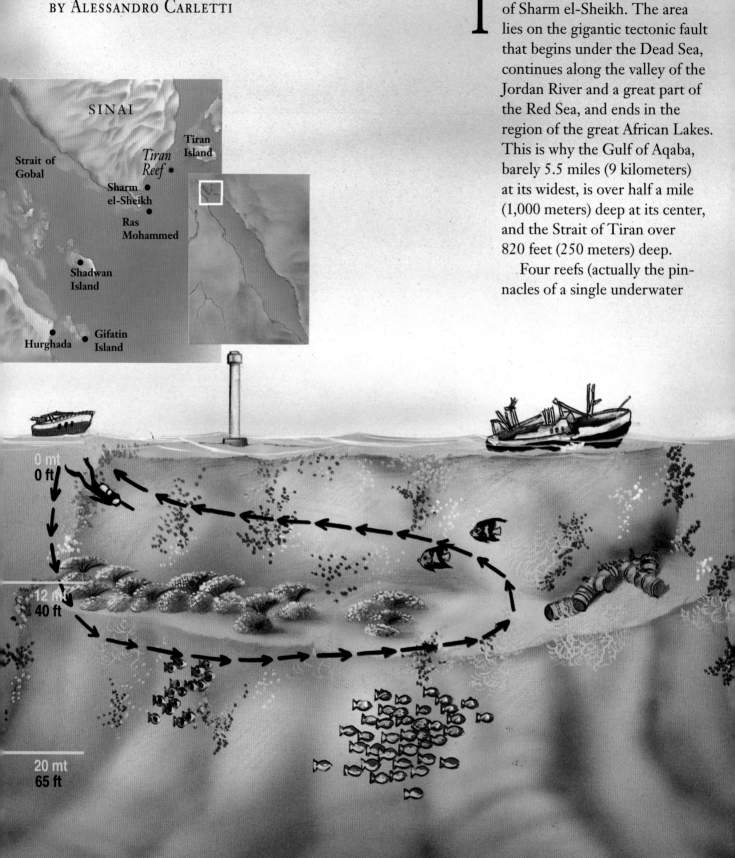

ridge) stretch lengthwise across the center of the strait. Their walls drop almost directly down to a depth of 200 feet (60 meters), and then plunge again into the midnight blue. Powerful currents sweep across the reef, heading southwest toward the open sea, so the walls accommodate an exceptional population of soft coral. Sightings of very large ocean fish, which must pass through the strait to enter or leave the gulf, are common.

Divers entering from the north will first encounter Jackson Reef; a huge freighter is grounded on

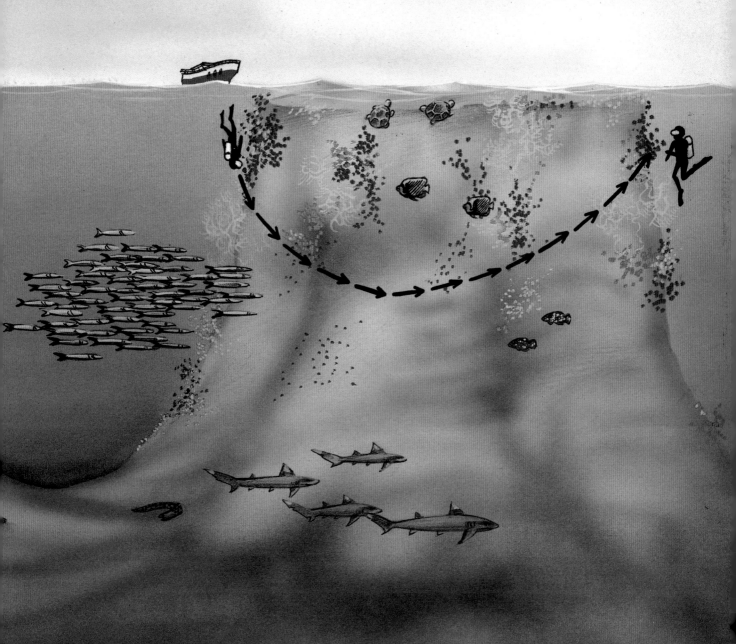

its northern side. It is forbidden to drop anchor anywhere in the maritime domain of Sharm el-Sheikh, but there are fixed moorings for dive boats on the southeast side, protected from the prevailing weather.

Divers head north, reaching depths between 16 and 98 feet (5 and 30 meters). Splendid gorgonian fans and soft corals adorn the rocks jutting out from the walls, and the flimsy green fronds of black coral dance in the currents. Orangespotted jack *(Carangoides bajad)* are constantly hunting, striking panic into the many species of smaller fish that live on the coral. When return-

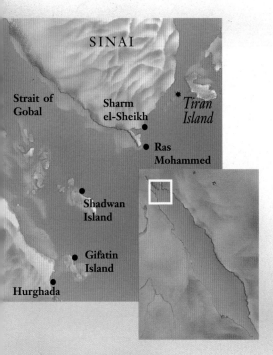

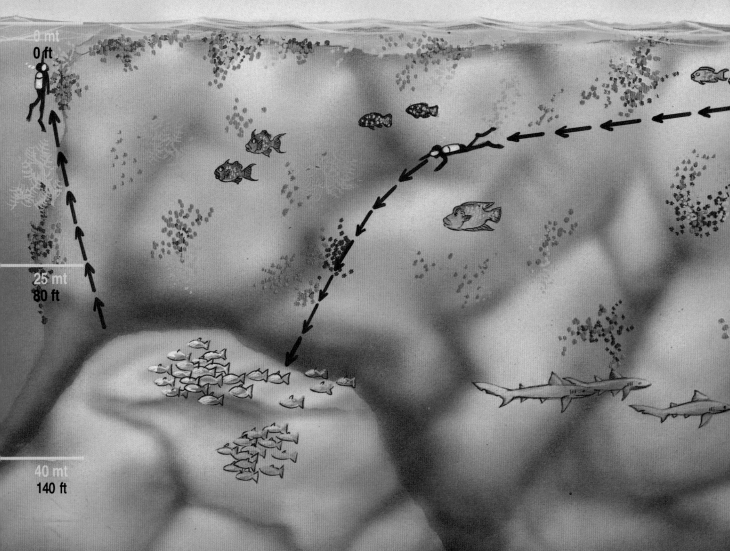

ing to the boat, divers glide through a garden of fire coral, umbrella-shaped acropora, and round formations of Favites and *Gonioporae* just below the surface. Sea turtles are frequently sighted on or near the surface, and tropical grunts and angelfish find peace in the sandy surface inlets. Gray sharks, whitetip reef sharks, eagle rays, and, in winter, manta rays, often pass in the deeper waters that separate Jackson Reef from Woodhouse Reef.

Woodhouse Reef is long and narrow, with sedimentary walls on which comparatively few varieties of coral live, since the walls are at a disadvantageous angle to

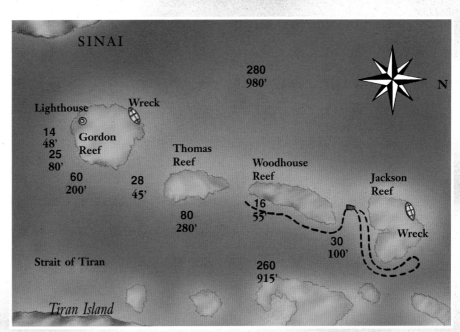

SINAI

280
980'

Lighthouse   Wreck

14
48'   Gordon
25   Reef   Thomas
80'   Reef   Woodhouse
60   28   Reef   Jackson
200'   45'   Reef

80   16
280'   55

260   30
915'   100'   Wreck

Strait of Tiran

Tiran Island

N

currents. There are no moorings, so it is best to dive north to south from a moving boat. A narrow canyon with a sandy bottom and a small satellite reef about 60 feet (18 meters) long with interesting grottoes and nooks has developed 120 feet (40 meters) down the eastern wall. Nurse sharks, easy to approach and photograph, are often sighted on the shelf that

E. Large gorgonians are common on the Gordon Reef. They tend to proliferate in very clear waters at a depth of less than 65 feet (20 meters).
PHOTOGRAPH BY ANDREA AND ANTONELLA FERRARI

F. Soft corals tend to grow on a rocky or coral base, on shallow seabeds where the sunlight still penetrates.
PHOTOGRAPH BY VINCENZO PAOLILLO

A

B

A. An aerial shot of the 4 reefs that lie before the Strait of Tiran. In the foreground is Gordon Reef, then Thomas Reef, Woodhouse Reef, and Jackson Reef.
PHOTOGRAPH BY ITAMAR GRINBERG

B. Thomas Reef has a remarkable concentration of soft corals, with a vast range of color, up to a depth of 65 feet (20 meters).
PHOTOGRAPH BY PIERFRANCO DILENGE

C. Along the wall of the reef, great gorgonian fans grow particularly well in the powerful sea currents.
PHOTOGRAPH BY GIANFRANCO D'AMATO

D. Great schools of barracuda (Sphyraena qenie) swim with the current.
PHOTOGRAPH BY PIERFRANCO DILENGE

runs the length of the reef at a depth of 98 feet (30 meters).

Thomas Reef is the smallest, but most colorful and exciting, of the 4. Its exposure and round shape make it extremely difficult to guess which way the current is flowing without first making a test dive, but it is worth the work. The northern extremity is a phantasmagoria of white, pink, orange, and purple soft corals, over which divers can swoop, pulled along by the current. The current will determine whether the dive is clockwise or counterclockwise, but it is nearly always possible to cover three-quarters of the circumference of the reef with the boat following the divers. This experience should be left to expert divers because of the violent currents. Unfortunately for less expert divers, on calm days

C

D

all the soft corals close their tentacles and appear to wither.

From Gordon Reef, the easternmost point on the Strait of Tiran, you can see the Cape Ras Nusrani lighthouse about 1 mile (1.6 kilometers) away on the Sinai coast. The dive boat mooring is not far from Gordon Reef's lighthouse, 165 feet (50 meters) away from the point where the reef breaks the surface, over a coral clearing 10 meters down. A great variety of coral fish swim among large formations of Favites and Porites, which look like giant coral "brains." Swim north and you will see dozens of old drums, the cargo of a grounded freighter, that have been appropriated by groupers and other sea creatures. Rarely, colonies of "garden eels" (*Heteroconger halis*) will emerge like slim, gray blades of grass from the sandy seabed about 15 feet (4 or 5 meters) deep to sway in the current, rapidly retreating at the slightest vibration. Whitetip reef sharks are a more common sight—some are permanent residents—and eagle rays swim not far from the eastern rim of the seabed, about 195 feet (60 meters) deep.

You may see large schools of bottlenose dolphins and, with luck, a few large pilot whales on the 90-minute ride back to Sharm el-Sheikh.

E
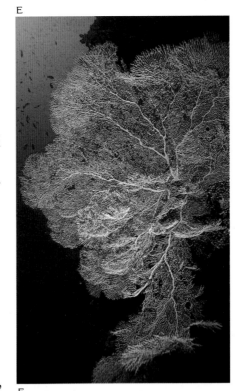

F

G

H

G. *A pair of butterfly-fish* (Chaetodon fasciatus) *swims in the clear waters on the seabeds of Tiran.*
PHOTOGRAPH BY VINCENZO PAOLILLO

H. *A group of crescent-tail bigeyes* (Priacanthus hamrur) *displays daytime coloration; by night, these fish change their color from bright red to silver.*
PHOTOGRAPH BY VINCENZO PAOLILLO

Ras Umm Sid

BY ALESSANDRO CARLETTI

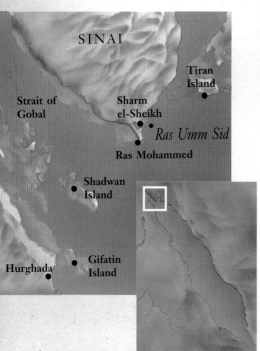

Ras Umm Sid, a promontory with a lighthouse just east of the harbor of Sharm el-Sheikh, is famous for its forest of giant gorgonians. These "octocorals," with extended fans designed to net passing plankton, thrive on the almost constant presence of the northern current.

Boats usually moor at the buoys set in the bay of Temple Reef, just outside the cape. Divers swim at a depth of about 50 feet (15 meters) along a shelf area, dense with coral and home to small coral fish, some groupers, and an occasional moray eel. Toward the point, the wall steepens and the floor drops away sharply. Large clumps of soft coral gather on the rocks most exposed to the currents—huge blooms of color among the darkness of the grottoes. The gorgonians cover an area of about 535 square feet (50 square meters) at depths ranging from 50 to 115 feet (15 to 35 meters). Small

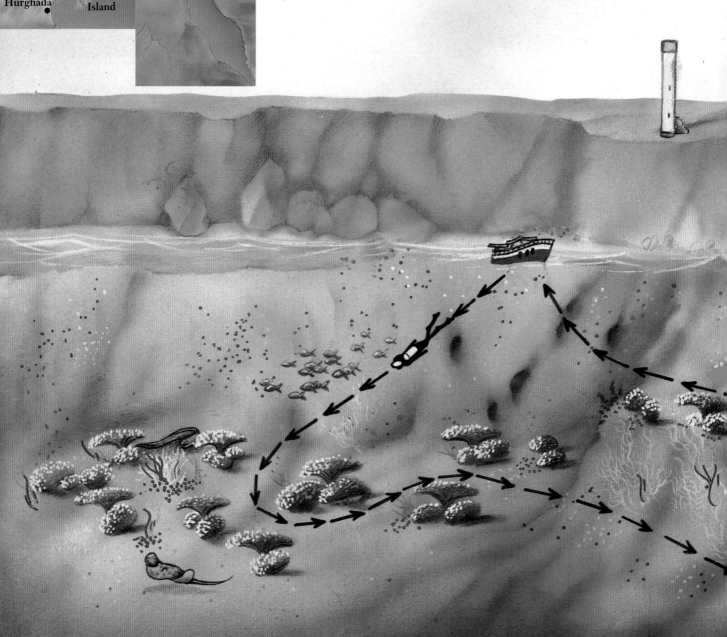

groupers, angelfish, red anthias, and vast schools of glassfish, small and transparent with gold highlights, swim among the fans.

When the sea is rough and the current strong, sail about 325 feet (100 meters) past the cape and dive without anchoring. From here, swim at an easy angle onto a vast coral shelf at 50 feet (15 meters) and on to reach the "upper" corals. The boat will follow you for a while and then wait at the permanent mooring.

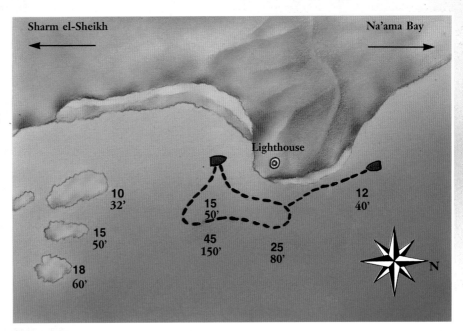

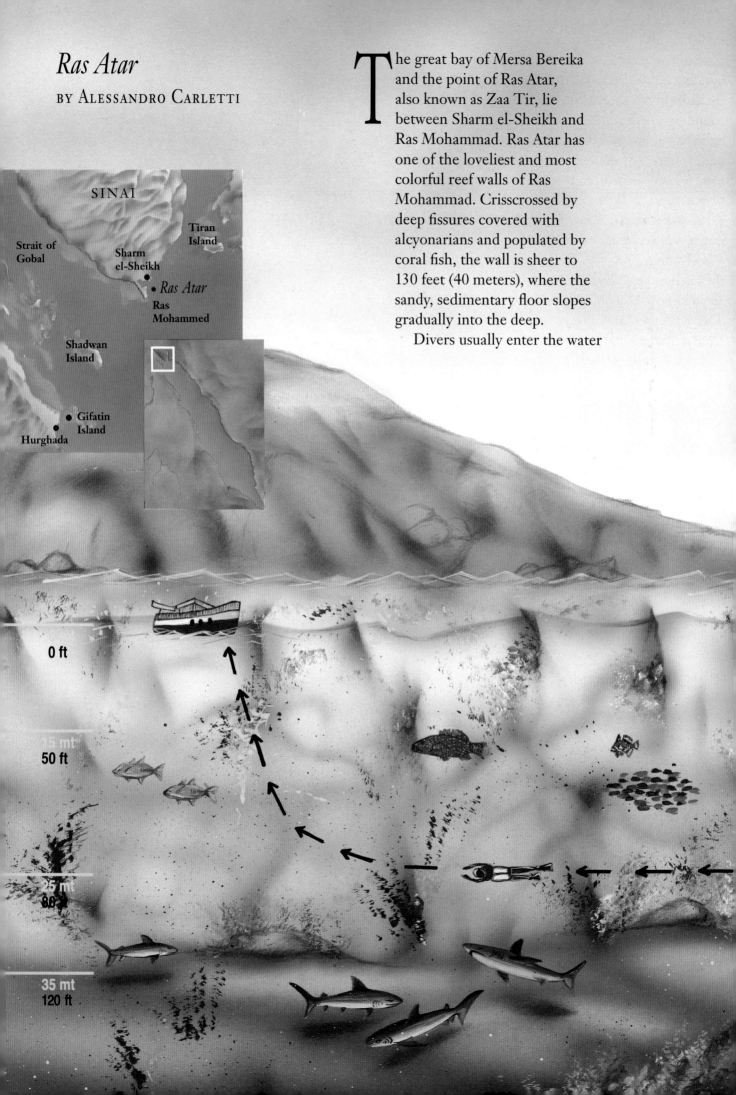

Ras Atar

BY ALESSANDRO CARLETTI

T he great bay of Mersa Bereika and the point of Ras Atar, also known as Zaa Tir, lie between Sharm el-Sheikh and Ras Mohammad. Ras Atar has one of the loveliest and most colorful reef walls of Ras Mohammad. Crisscrossed by deep fissures covered with alcyonarians and populated by coral fish, the wall is sheer to 130 feet (40 meters), where the sandy, sedimentary floor slopes gradually into the deep.

Divers usually enter the water

SINAI

Tiran Island

Strait of Gobal

Sharm el-Sheikh

Ras Atar

Ras Mohammed

Shadwan Island

Gifatin Island

Hurghada

0 ft

15 mt
50 ft

25 mt
80 ft

35 mt
120 ft

from a boat about 330 feet (100 meters) inside the bay and allow the current to carry them out, rounding the point of the cape and continuing to Ras Mohammad. There are plenty of passing fish-jacks (*Caranx* sp.), small tuna (*Thunnus* sp.), whitetip reef sharks (*Triaenodon obesus*), and, deeper down, shortnose blacktail sharks (*Carcharhinus wheeleri*). When the current is powerful, the alcyonarians swell and bloom. This is an excellent dive to do from a moving boat.

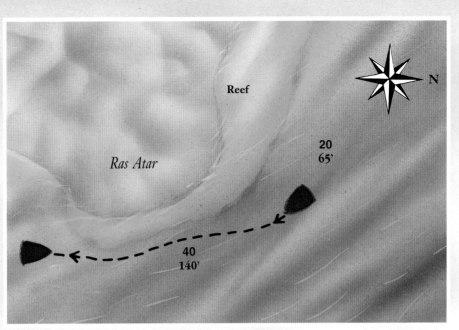

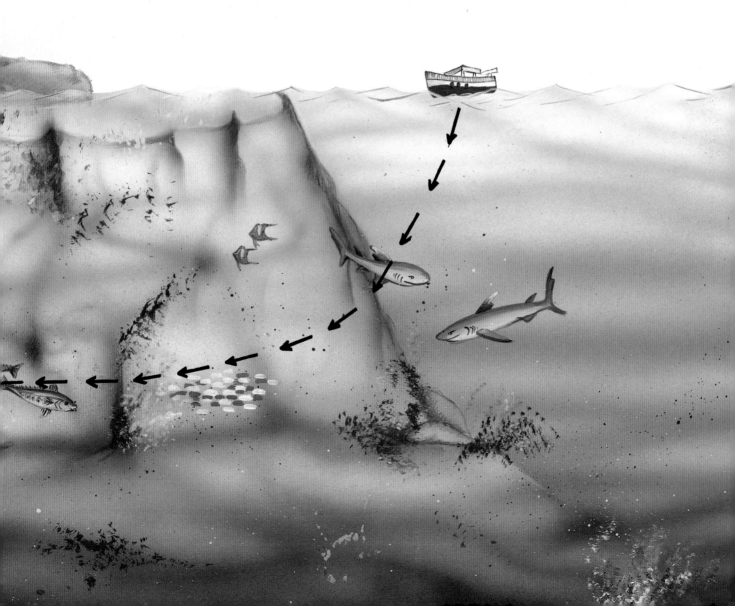

Ras Mohammad

BY ALESSANDRO
CARLETTI

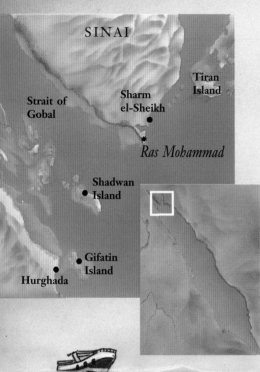

Ras Mohammad, the cape that forms the southernmost tip of the Sinai, is probably the best known dive site in the Red Sea. The promontory, which includes the Black Hill, is connected to dry land by a slender strip of sand, on the eastern side of which is the huge bay of Mersa Bareika. Ras Mohammad has 2 rocky tips: a high one to the east, known as the Shark Observatory, and a lower one to the west, off of which lie the famous reefs that break the water's dark surface here and there.

The Black Hill was declared a national park in 1989. Divers at the site must follow a specific set of rules (available at the Sharm el-Sheikh tourist office), including these basics:

- Do not drop anchor on the reef.
- Do not gather live or fossilized coral.
- Do not feed the fish.

Gray sharks, barracuda, snappers, jacks, tuna, humphead wrasses, moray eels, and coral fish swim the underwater garden of multicolored soft corals and giant gorgonians at Ras Mohammad. From here, you will be looking out over the East African

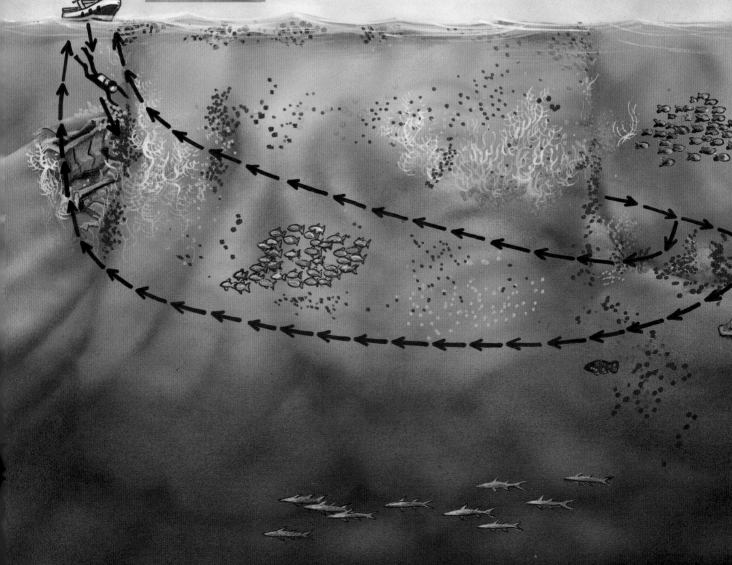

tectonic trench, almost half a mile (800 meters) deep at this point. Because of the currents that sweep out from the Gulf of Aqaba, many ocean fish species gather here in search of food and shelter.

In the central area there is a coastal reef, which encloses a vast lagoon along the beach and then drops in a gentle saddle ranging from 15 to 80 feet (5 to 15 meters) deep. The 2 huge coral towers of Jolanda Reef (west) and Shark Reef (east) rise from this.

The outer wall of Shark Reef drops straight down and is almost constantly pounded by heavy

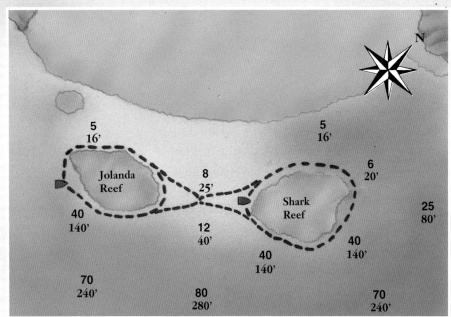

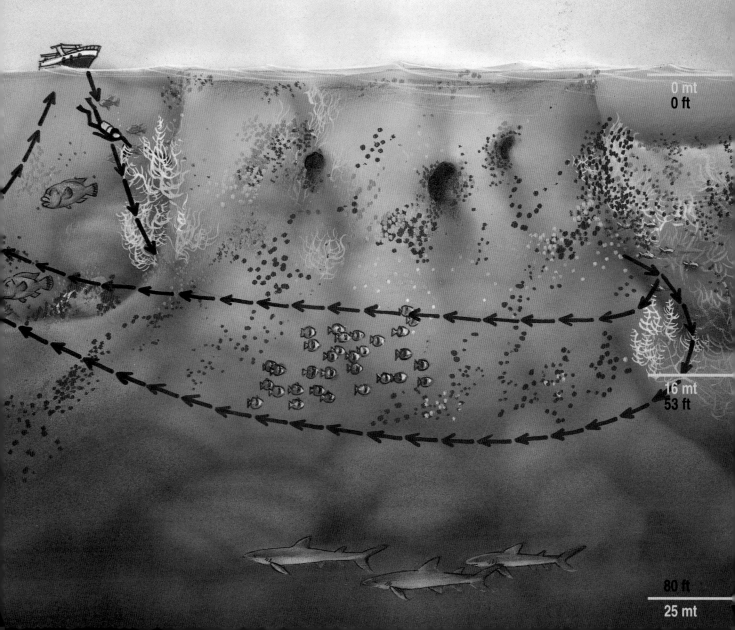

currents. Divers set out from the saddle between the 2 reefs (where large humphead wrasses and giant moral eels live permanently), swim counterclockwise around Shark Reef, and then pull themselves against the current along specially installed cables until they reach the thrilling drop into the deep. Astonishingly large gorgonians grow on the left-hand wall. One of the best known sights of Ras Mohammad is a large school of huge snappers that often gathers here, in the center of the channel that separates this area from Shark Reef.

The northern current that you were just pulling against will now help you along the circular route of the dive. On one side, you will see the wall of soft corals thronged with tiny red *Anthias squamipinnis;* on the other, the blue depths, from which at any moment a shark or a

A

B

C

barracuda might appear. The dive ends where it started, between the 2 towers, protected from the current. The rare absence of the northern current allows a more relaxing dive, but also a less interesting one, with fewer of the creatures that come to feed on the current's constant stream of plankton and microscopic animals.

The route around Jolanda Reef is not as deep, and its outer wall are less steep for a considerable stretch, though eventually it too drops into deep water. Again, dives should go counterclockwise here.

The reef got its name from the wrecked freighter *Jolanda,* which sank there after a violent storm in 1981. The remains of the hull lie 650 feet (200 meters) under, but

D

E

F

E. A gray reef shark (Carcharhinus amblyrhynchos) swims by the photographer. Although sharks have diminished considerably in number, it is possible to encounter a few in these waters, especially in the winter when there are relatively few tourists.
PHOTOGRAPH BY
FRANCO BANFI

F. Humphead wrasses (Cheilinus undulatus) are now considered one of the distinctive features at Ras Mohammad. Adult specimens may be longer than 6.5 feet (2 meters).
PHOTOGRAPH BY
GIANFRANCO D'AMATO

G. Impenetrable schools of bigeye trevallies (Caranx sexfasciatus) illuminate the depths of the sea with flashes of light.
PHOTOGRAPH BY
MARCELLO BERTINETTI

G

H

H. The proliferation of soft corals in the Red Sea has been described as "living upholstery."
PHOTOGRAPH BY
GIANFRANCO D'AMATO

other debris is found on the reef, including 2 broken bathroom-fixture containers that are now dens for angelfish, grunts, and bluespotted stingrays. The eastern side is dotted with many colorful corals, though gorgonians are almost completely absent.

Divers have yet another treat in store at Ras Mohammad. About 330 feet (100 meters) northeast of Shark Reef, just under the tip of the cape, is a shelf ranging in depth from 50 to 65 feet (16 to 20 meters), known as "Anemone City." An astounding number of huge anemones, surrounded by dozens of twobar anemonefish and domino fish, thrive in an area just under 1,100 square feet (100 square meters). Such an intense gathering of Actiniaria is found nowhere else on earth and is a mystery to biologists.

Beacon Rock: Wreck of the Dunraven

BY ALESSANDRO CARLETTI

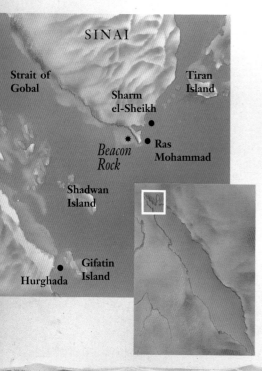

An hour's sail west of Ras Moham-mad is the huge, surface-breaking reef of Beacon Rock. Marked by a lighthouse, Beacon Rock is the farthest tip of Sha'ab Mahmud, the large coral reef that extends 6 miles (10 kilometers) to the northwest, almost touching the coast of western Sinai. Waters murky from sediment stirred up by northern winds and forma-tions of *Goniopora*, Porites, and Favites give the reefs in this area a rounded but comparatively

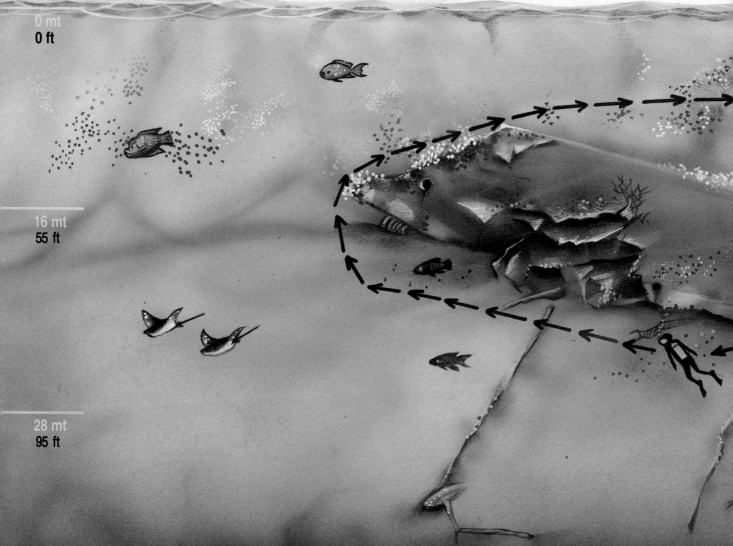

0 mt
0 ft

16 mt
55 ft

28 mt
95 ft

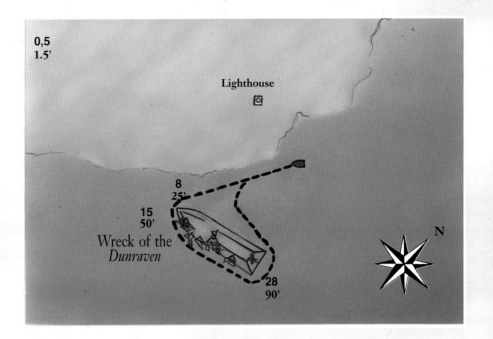

0,5
1.5'

Lighthouse

8
25'

15
50'

Wreck of the
Dunraven

28
90'

N

A

B

C

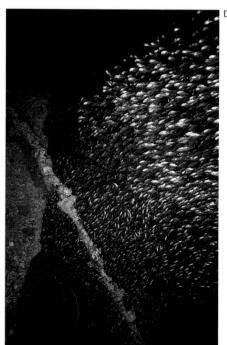

D

A. The Dunraven, *an English steamer heading for the East Indies, met its tragic fate on Beacon Rock in 1876. The wreck was discovered by the Israelis in 1978. Here you can see the rudder and the huge propeller.*
PHOTOGRAPH BY
ANDREA GHISOTTI

B. One of Dunraven's *masts, now encrusted with coral. You can see the crow's nest and part of the rigging.*
PHOTOGRAPH BY
ANDREA GHISOTTI

C. The impact against the reef and the continuous currents have scattered the remains of the wreck across the seabed.
PHOTOGRAPH BY
ANDREA GHISOTTI

D. Silvery clouds of glassfish (Parapriacanthus guentheri) *cast light on the contorted beams of the hold.*
PHOTOGRAPH BY
ANDREA GHISOTTI

colorless appearance. There are humphead wrasses (less sociable than those at Ras Mohammad), many oopuhue *(Tetraodon hispidus)*, pufferfish, and tropical groupers. It is not uncommon to spot sea turtles close to the surface or the occasional eagle ray. The only sharks ever sighted at Beacon Rock are whitetip reef sharks, which swim along peacefully and hasten away timidly when disturbed.

The *Dunraven*, an English steamer built in Newcastle around 1870, sank in 1876 at Beacon Rock on the way back from the

Indies with a cotton and wool cargo. Its starboard side struck the reef, ripping 3 large holes, and then it sank after fire broke out. It overturned and settled 230 feet (60 meters) down, where it was discovered 100 years later by Israeli scuba divers.

Divers can easily swim toward the wreck from the permanent mooring at the tip of Beacon Rock. At 90 feet (28 meters) the stern, pointing toward the surface, comes into view, its huge screw and rudder decked with soft corals. The entire keel is practically intact and is thoroughly covered with coral. Divers can enter the hull through one of the gashes on the starboard side; the interior is dark and the bottom covered with sand, mud, and

E

detritus. Many large groupers have chosen the wreck as their home, and the huge coal boiler in the central area now shimmers with tiny glassfish swimming in shafts of light. At the prow, about 52 feet (16 meters) below the surface, the anchor chain dangles; the anchor itself is far away on the reef. On the seabed, stretching out toward open sea, are bits and pieces of the deck and the 2 masts, one still with its crow's nest. To end the dive, swim up the wall of the reef to make your way back to the mooring.

F

G

E. The screw of the Dunraven *appears totally transfigured by coral encrustations.*
PHOTOGRAPH BY ANDREA GHISOTTI

F. Many groupers live in the structures of the wreck. In this picture, you can see a coral grouper (Cephalopholis miniata).
PHOTOGRAPH BY PAOLO FOSSATI

G. It is fairly common to encounter sea turtles (Eretmochelys imbricata) near the wreck.
PHOTOGRAPH BY ANDREA GHISOTTI

Alternative Reef

BY ALESSANDRO CARLETTI

Three miles west of Ras Moham-mad, the system of coral towers known as Alternative Reef is actually the southernmost tip of Sha'ab el Utaf Reef, which stretches from the western coast of Sinai. All the towers make good dive sites, but the largest one (second from the east) has the richest and most colorful fish and coral; it also has a small satellite reef to explore on its southeastern side. From the mooring on the northern edge, about 165 feet (50 meters) from the peak, divers can easily travel around the reef to see the spectacular southern ridge, where saber squirrelfish (*Adioryx spinifer*), glassfish, angelfish, and butterflyfish search for food among the lavish gorgonians, red and green sea whip corals, and hard and soft corals.

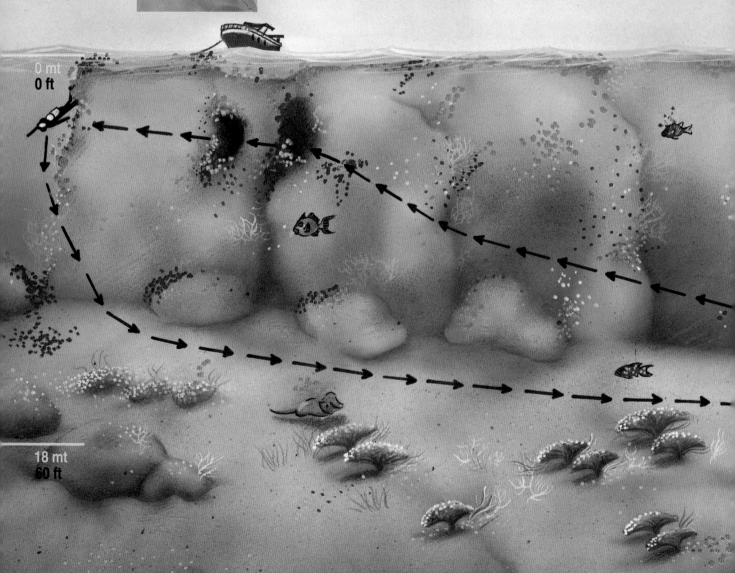

The route is easy, with a maximum depth of 60 feet (18 meters) and waters that are almost always calm, so a night dive is definitely recommended. By night, many pufferfish sleep in "nests" of soft coral, and the coral-eating crown of thorns starfish (*Acanthaster lanci*), splendid sea lilies, and pencil urchins make their appearance.

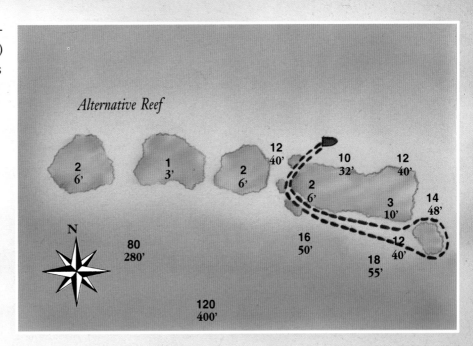

Alternative Reef

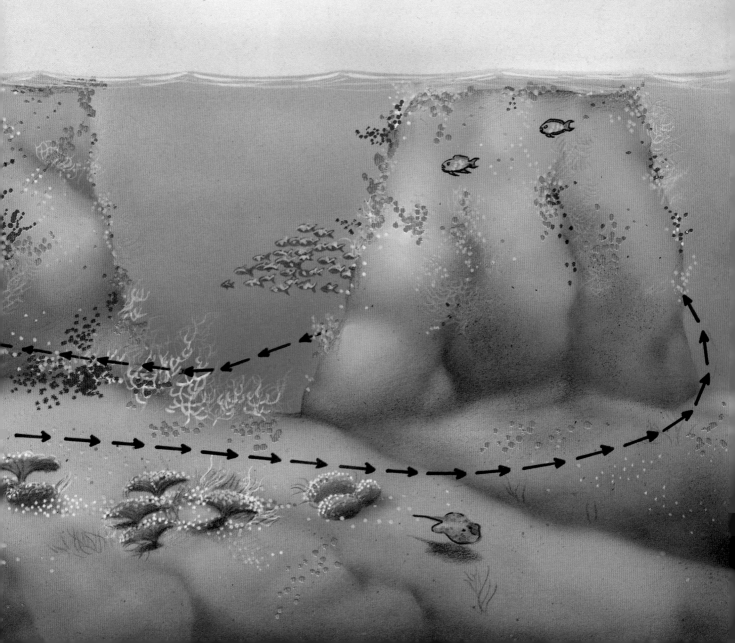

Stingray Station

BY ALESSANDRO CARLETTI

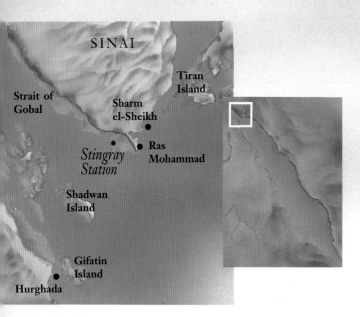

S tingray Station is the last coral tower of Alternative Reef, on the southeast side of Sha'ab el-Utaf. Daily boats from Sharm el-Sheikh and cruise boats take divers to this exceptional site, which takes its name from an intense population of bluespotted stingrays *(Taeniura lymma)*. Few tourists come here, so reef life is undisturbed. The inner wall slopes onto a broad, sandy lagoon rarely deeper than 50 feet (15 meters). The western wall is deeper and has all the lush underwater life characteristic of Alternative Reef.

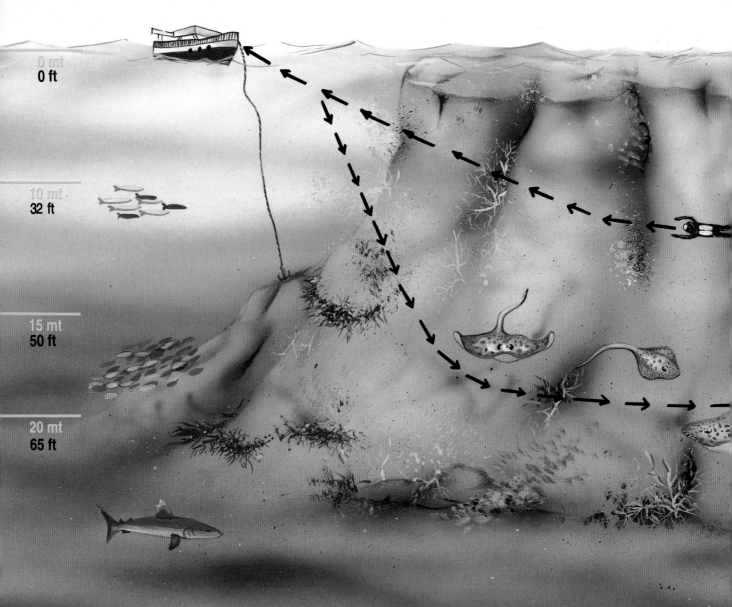

Dive boats moor at a "dead anchor" on the side facing the open sea. Visibility can be less than perfect: wave action from the Suez Canal and the reef's marked exposure to the open sea often stir up the sandy floor, which is deeper and more variable than in reefs located farther east. Sea turtles, eagle rays, and bluespotted stingrays can be found with the ever-present humphead wrasses, and microfauna populate the reef at night—sea urchins, crinoids, lobsters, sea stars, camouflaged polyps, crabs, and nudibranches.

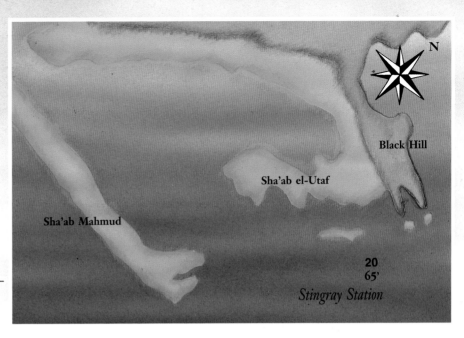

Black Hill

Sha'ab el-Utaf

Sha'ab Mahmud

20
65'
Stingray Station

N

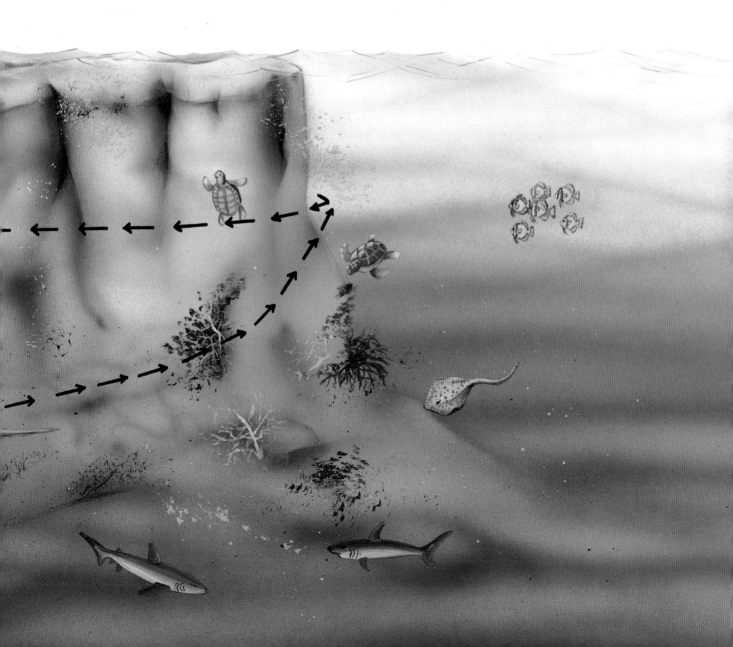

Sha'ab Ali: Wreck of *the* Thistlegorm

BY ALESSANDRO CARLETTI

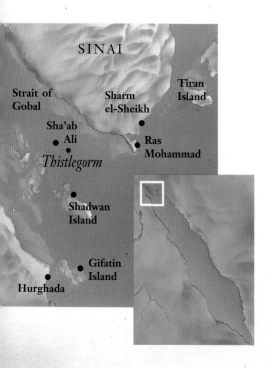

SINAI

Strait of Gobal

Sharm el-Sheikh

Tiran Island

Sha'ab Ali

Thistlegorm

Ras Mohammad

Shadwan Island

Gifatin Island

Hurghada

Jacques-Yves Cousteau discovered this wreck in 1956, during one of the first expeditions of the *Calypso*. It lies on a sandy seabed 90 feet (28 meters) deep and a few miles to the north of Shag Rock, the southern tip of the great reef of Sha'ab Ali in the Gulf of Suez.

The S.S. *Thistlegorm* was built in the English shipyards of Joseph Thompson and Sons in 1940. It was intended to transport war material as part of an Allied offensive to relaunch the Eighth Army against Rommel. The 49 crew members were waiting for the reopening of the Suez Canal (which had been rendered

0 mt

0 ft

28 mt

90 ft

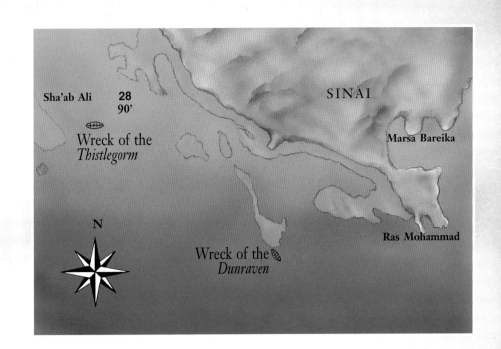

Sha'ab Ali **28**
           90'

Wreck of the
Thistlegorm

SINAI

Marsa Bareika

Ras Mohammad

N

Wreck of the
Dunraven

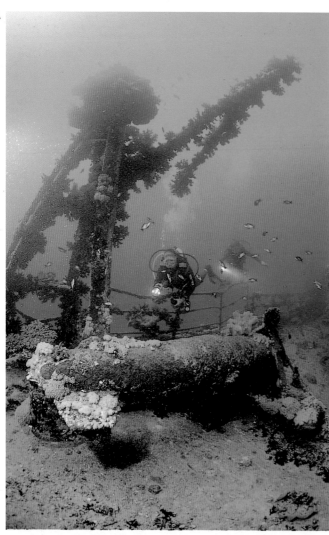

inoperative by attack), had sailed around Africa, put in briefly at Aden, and were on their way up the Red Sea when the Germans bombed them in October 1941. Only 9 crew members were killed, but the vessel's stern section was destroyed when the cargo of ammunition exploded, and the ship sank.

The 9,000-ton hull is in sailing position, and the superstructure reaches to 40 feet (12 meters), which can be a help to divers looking for the surface in murky waters. The ship's considerable cargo is still virtually intact, making this wreck dive an eerie voy-

A. The anti-aircraft gun of the Thistlegorm.
PHOTOGRAPH BY ITAMAR GRINBERG

age into the past. Two large torpedoes and 4 railroad cars are on the main deck. Despite the silt and corrosion, automobiles, trucks carrying BSA and Norton motorcycles, jeeps, tires, tank tracks, and uniforms and boots for the troops can be made out clearly. Much of the equipment has been removed from the central deck, but portside of the hull, the stern is surrounded by plenty of material from the hold: towing equipment, 2 tanks, boxed ammunitions, and weapons. On the

B. A number of BSA motorcycles are still lined up perfectly in the hold of the freighter.
PHOTOGRAPH BY ANDREA AND ANTONELLA FERRARI

C. One of the 20 trucks carried by the freighter seems to be intact under the sedimentary silt of the Gulf of Suez.
PHOTOGRAPH BY ITAMAR GRINBERG

stern deck there is a 4-inch anti-aircraft gun, now pointing uselessly toward the seabed. Inside the ship, divers can explore the crew's quarters.

This wreck takes at least 2 dives, starting from the bow and proceeding to the stern, to explore fully.

D. Glassfish glitter in the structures of the wreck.
PHOTOGRAPH BY ITAMAR GRINBERG

E. The most common encounters about the wrecks in this area are with groupers. Here, an enormous Malabar grouper lurks in the Thistlegorm.
PHOTOGRAPH BY PAOLO FOSSATI

F. Diving onto a wreck is always an exciting experience; diving onto the Thistlegorm *is particularly thrilling because the cargo is still virtually intact.*
PHOTOGRAPH BY ITAMAR GRINBERG

G. The entire freighter and a considerable portion of its cargo are covered with thick undersea growth. Here are some more motorcycles.
PHOTOGRAPH BY ANDREA AND ANTONELLA FERRARI

H. The cargo of military materials stowed in the ship's 3 holds includes torpedoes, bombs, ammunition, trucks, motorcycles, tanks, locomotives, uniforms, and more.
PHOTOGRAPH BY ITAMAR GRINBERG

Bluff Point

BY ALESSANDRO CARLETTI

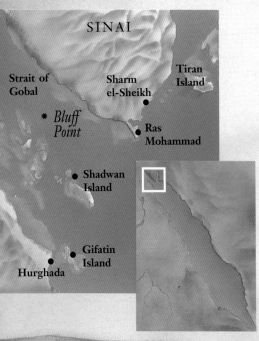

Kebira (Big Gobal) and Seghira (Little Gobal) are 2 islands on the western side of the Strait of Gobal at the mouth of the Suez Canal. Bluff Point, on Little Gobal, marks the exit and entrance to the gulf with an automatic lighthouse powered by solar panels.

Divers enter the water from a boat anchored in the shelter of the great bay and follow the coastal reef on the right out to the point. The maximum depth of 115 feet (35 meters) is reached under the lighthouse. There is a remarkable proliferation of hard and soft corals just under the surface, with little grottoes populated by small coral fish, and numerous black corals (Antipatharia) grow 80 feet (25 meters) down on the wall of Bluff Point. Sea turtles come here to hunt the small crustaceans and mollusks on the reef and to lay their eggs on the island in the spring. You will probably see some bottlenose dolphins, members of a large school that lives permanently off the Gobal Islands.

There is the wreck of a hull, probably from an Egyptian gunboat that went down during the

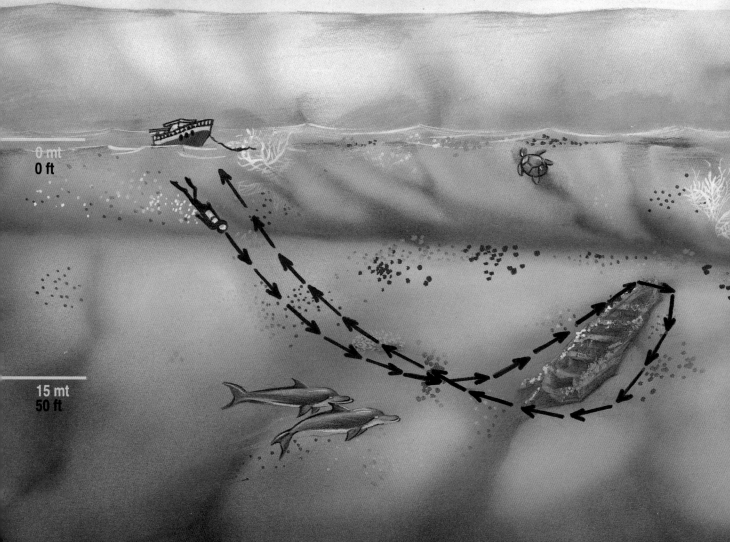

War of Independence, at 65 feet (20 meters) under the center of the bay. This makes a great night dive—red and orange soft corals hang from the ship's structures and you can see moray eels, scorpionfish, lionfish (the most venomous in the Red Sea), nudibranches, and crinoids.

Another wreck, badly damaged and covered with corals, lies 980 feet (300 meters) beyond the lighthouse on the northern side of the island. This freighter was carrying electrical material when it sank, and is now home to some of the reef's plentiful fauna.

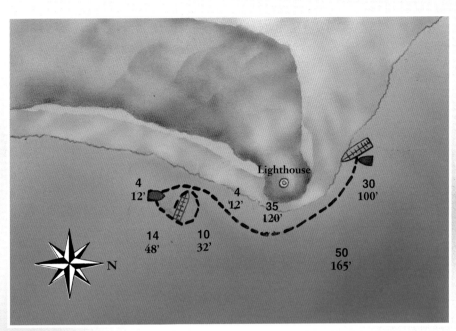

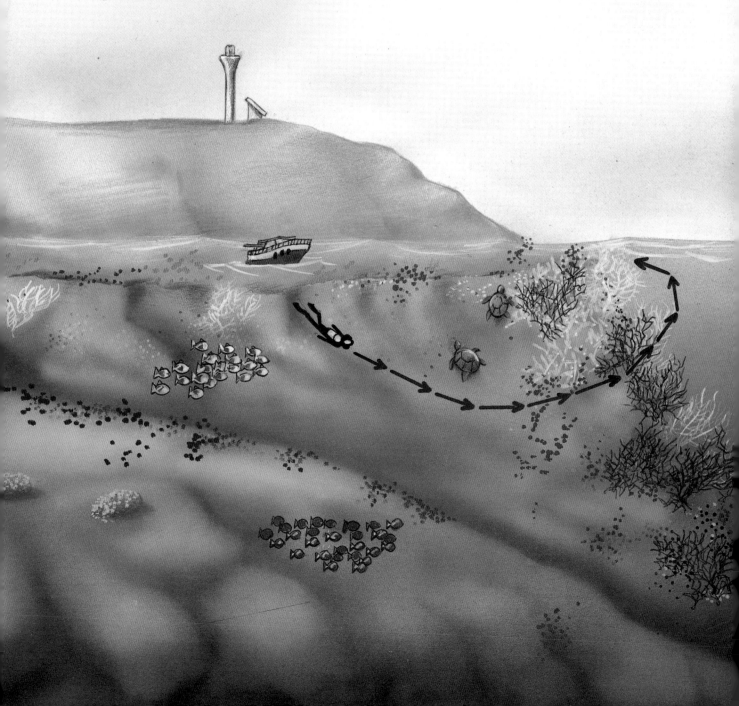

Sha'ab Abu Nuhâs: *Wrecks of the* Carnatic *and* Ghiannis D.

BY ALESSANDRO CARLETTI

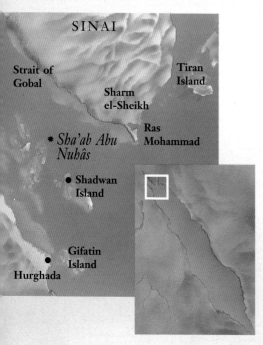

The great reef of Sha'ab Abu Nuhâs emerges 2 miles (3.5 kilometers) north of Shadwan Island at the mouth of the Strait of Gobal. A menace to navigation, the reef is infamous among sailors and celebrated by scuba divers. There are no fewer than 7 sunken ships from different eras on the seabeds, the *Carnatic* and the *Ghiannis D.* being the most intriguing.

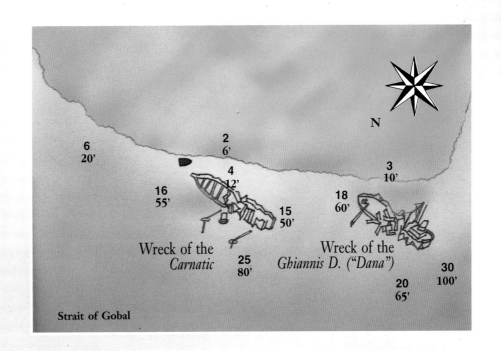

6
20'

2
6'

3
10'

4
12'

16
55'

18
60'

15
50'

N

Wreck of the
Carnatic

Wreck of the
Ghiannis D. ("Dana")

25
80'

30
100'

20
65'

Strait of Gobal

A. On the flattened poop of the Carnatic you can make out huge windows on the covered deck, the large rudder, and the 3-blade screw.
PHOTOGRAPH BY ANDREA GHISOTTI

B. A scuba diver swims through the remains of the first-class deck.
PHOTOGRAPH BY ANDREA GHISOTTI

C. The prow of the Carnatic appears to be completely covered with coral formations and stupendous soft corals.
PHOTOGRAPH BY ANDREA GHISOTTI

The *Carnatic*, a splendid 295-foot (90-meter) steamer, was sailing the Indies route for Bombay with a cargo of wine and "London soda water" when it collided against the reef on the night of September 13, 1869. It sank the following morning, settling on one side with the bow at 50 feet (16 meters) and the stern at 80 feet (24 meters). The deck faces the open sea, and the blackened support structures are clearly visible from the surface. The windowed quarterdeck, the large screw at the stern, and the giant ring and bowsprit supports at the prow are particularly impressive. The keel is virtually intact, but the wooden components and much of the navigating

equipment are long gone. You can see numerous bottles of wine, engraved with a large "No. 2" and still sealed with corks, in the forward hold along with the distinctive oval soda bottles made of transparent opaline glass. The sea floor in front of the wreck is strewn with the remains of the smokestack, the masts, and other debris.

It is best to dive the *Carnatic* in the morning because visibility can be poor: the currents over the sandy bottom are strong and the blackened wreck, having a northern exposure, is shaded by the walls of the reef for most of the day.

The *Ghiannis D.*, a large, modern freighter, sank 200 feet (60 meters) and is slightly to the south of the *Carnatic*. The wreck is referred to as the *Dana*, because of the huge "D" (for the Danae Shipping Company) that can be seen on the smokestack. Its original name, *Markos*, disappeared after years of corrosion. After hitting the reef head on, the ship remained grounded for 6 weeks before it sank slowly to the seabed. The wreck's deepest point is 90 feet (28 meters). The hull was shattered at 3 points by violent wave action. The bow and stern remain intact, but the central holds have been destroyed, and only rusted sheet metal, cables, and pipes remain of the ship's cargo. Divers should swim first toward the prow, where the anchor chain drapes onto the reef, and then swim back toward the stern. Inside the stern, the command bridge, residential quarters, and engine room offer a series of impressive tours. Groupers have taken up residence in the central section of the boat, and jacks, snappers, eagle rays, and sharks are frequent passersby.

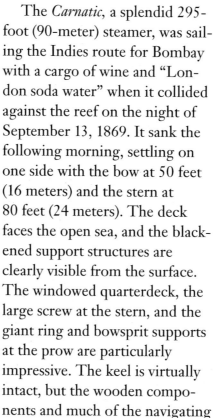

D

E

F

D. The large "D" that appears on the smokestack refers to the Danae Shipping Company.
<small>PHOTOGRAPH BY ANDREA GHISOTTI</small>

E. The stern section of the Ghiannis D. *lies intact on the sand at 82 feet (25 meters), while the holds appear to have been completely destroyed.*
<small>PHOTOGRAPH BY ANDREA GHISOTTI</small>

F. Metal structures in the area of the quarter-deck on the Ghiannis D. *stand out clearly against the transparent water.*
<small>PHOTOGRAPH BY ANDREA GHISOTTI</small>

G. A great barracuda (Sphyraena barracuda) *swims majestically across the deck.*
<small>PHOTOGRAPH BY VINCENZO PAOLILLO</small>

G

Siyul Kebira Island

BY ALESSANDRO CARLETTI

This island, distinguished by low coral rocks and a solar-powered lighthouse, can be reached in 2 hours by boat from Hurghada. It offers one of the finest and least crowded dives on the western shore of the Strait of Gobal, especially suitable for beginners.

The lagoon off the southern side, no deeper than 80 feet (25 meters) and with a reflective coral floor, has the most interesting features and the best light. Angelfish, butterflyfish, red anthias, and tiny bluegreen chromis take shelter there under the beautiful and varied acropora

formations. Bottom-dwelling sharks are a frequent sight and there are plenty of passing fish, especially during the winter. It is a good idea to coast along the eastern shore by boat for a few hundred yards and then to swim with the southwest current.

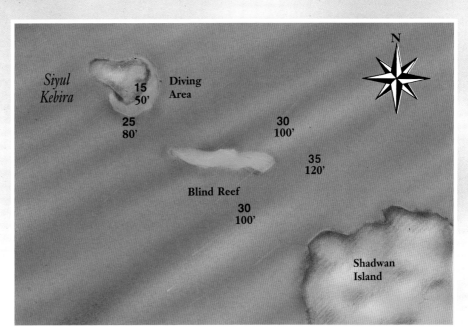

Blind Reef

BY ALESSANDRO CARLETTI

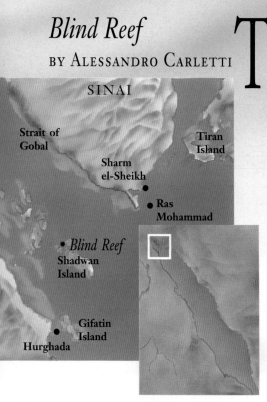

This long narrow reef, midway between the islands of Shadwan and Siyul Kebira, is a good place to shelter when sailing from Hurghada toward the Gobal Islands. Its barrier reef protects a broad area from the constant north wind, and its 2 extremities offer excellent dives. The reef is shaded from the sun most of the day, so it is best to dive in the full morning light.

At the southeast point, after a short stretch of steep wall, divers can move along a broad slope at a depth of between 70 and 150 feet (20 and 45 meters). The sandy seabed is crossed by long ribs of beautiful coral formations. There is a spectacular concentration of red sea whips, reaching straight up from the sea floor in 2 points, and many black coral formations, some of them very

large, rising treelike from 115 feet (35 meters). Eagle rays, manta rays, and plenty of pelagic fish live undisturbed here. You are most likely to see gray sharks, which frequent Shadwan Island, and sea turtles that appear at the surface.

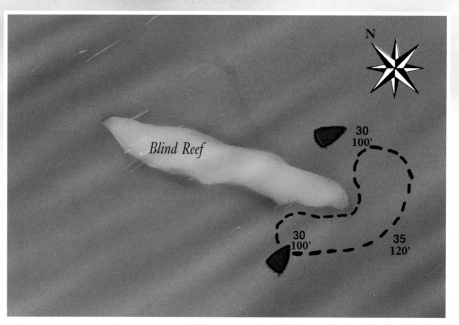

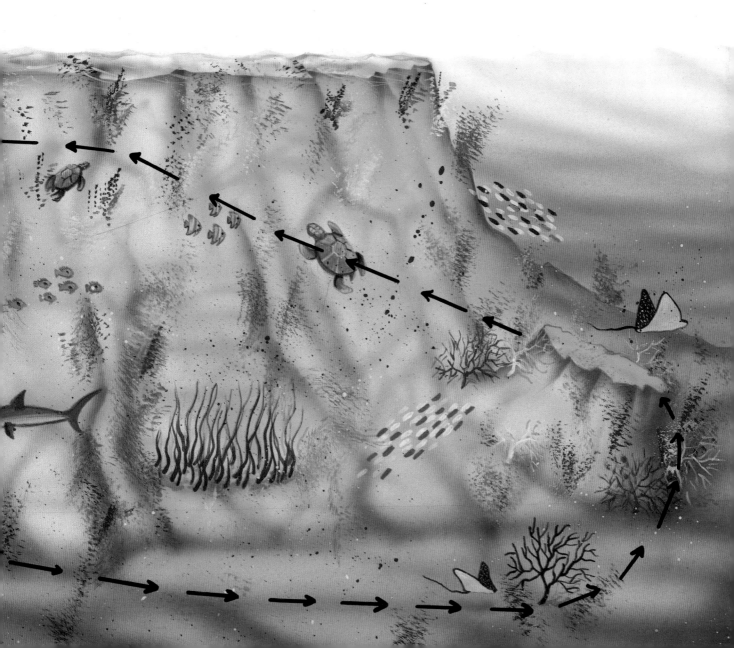

Umm Gamar Island

BY ALESSANDRO CARLETTI

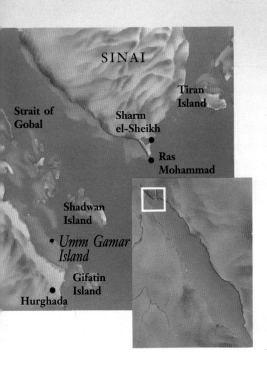

This is the most popular and the northernmost dive in the Hurghada archipelago. Umm Gamar is the kingdom of poisonous fish and attracts dozens of divers every day. The vast littoral reef stretches to the south, narrowing considerably around the rest of the island's perimeter.

Dives are made onto a slope that drops gently from 50 feet (15 meters) to 250 feet (75 meters). The reef wall is adorned with handsome alcyonarians; its many nooks and crannies are

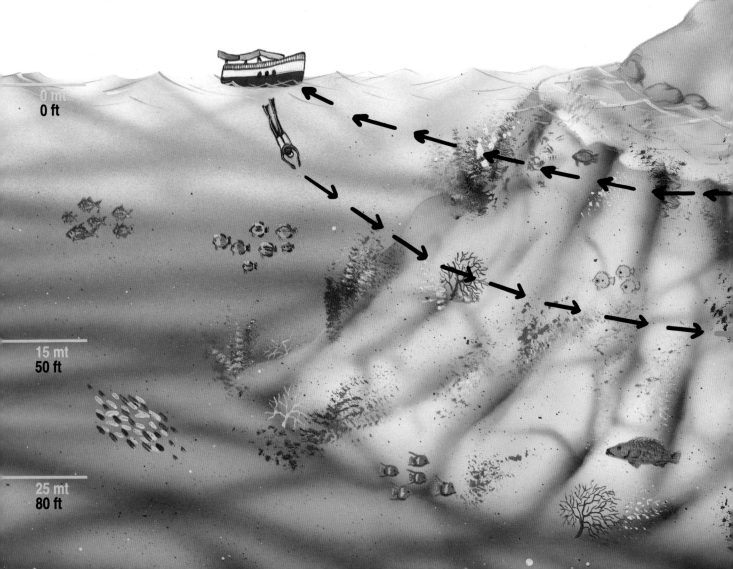

0 mt
0 ft

15 mt
50 ft

25 mt
80 ft

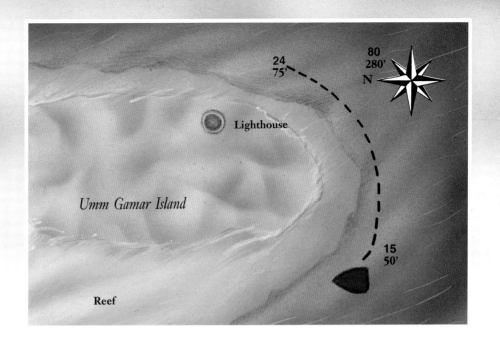

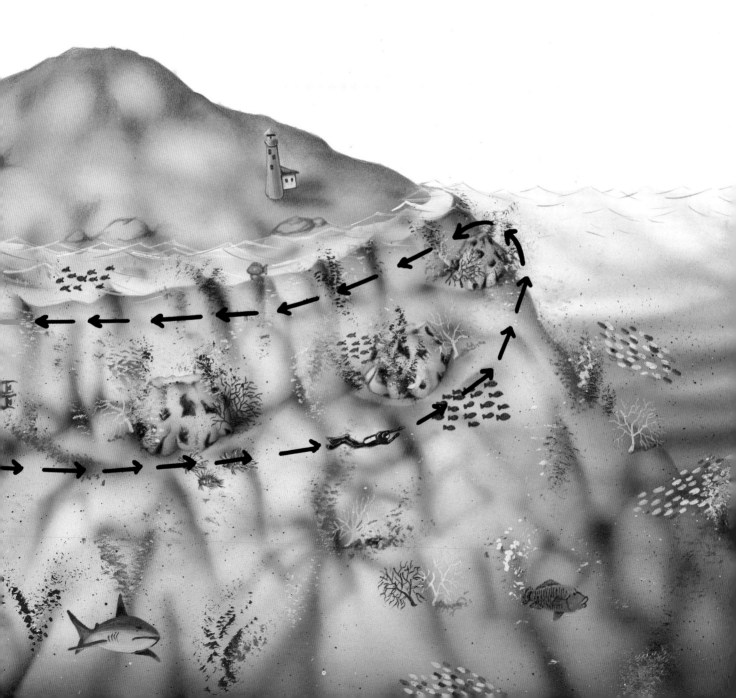

home to coral fish that have become accustomed to the heavy diver traffic. There are 3 tall coral formations to the east, 2 at 66 feet (20 meters) and 1 at 33 feet (10 meters). Each one is hollow and inside you can see families of turkeyfish, false stonefish, and, camouflaged along the walls, devil scorpionfish. There are swarms of glassfish everywhere, and if you look carefully you may see a stonefish *(Synanceia verrucosa)* blending perfectly with the seabed.

All of these species, except the glassfish, are dangerous, armed with poisonous spines that can be lethal. Wear gloves and make sure not to brush up against anything.

A

B

C

A. A scorpionfish (Scorpaenopsis barbatus), *one of the most dangerous inhabitants of the reef of Umm Gamar, rests on the seabed.*
PHOTOGRAPH BY VINCENZO PAOLILLO

B. A bluespotted lagoon ray (Taeniura lymma), *partly covered in sand, blends in with the seabed.*
PHOTOGRAPH BY VINCENZO PAOLILLO

C. A number of splendid pink sea whips reach for the surface.
PHOTOGRAPH BY SERGIO QUAGLIA

D

D. A pair of giant morays (Gymnothorax javanicus) *survey their territory, peering out of the safe haven of their den.*
PHOTOGRAPH BY
VINCENZO PAOLILLO

E. A pink alcyonarian stands out in all its majesty against the blue surface.
PHOTOGRAPH BY
FRANCO BANFI

F. Acanthaster planci *like this one, with their razor-sharp spines, devour coral polyps and destroy great stretches of coral reef.*
PHOTOGRAPH BY
VINCENZO PAOLILLO

G. Some blackspotted grunts (Plectorhynchus gaterinus) *hover near the reef.*
PHOTOGRAPH BY
VINCENZO PAOLILLO

E

F

G

H

H. The lionfish (Pterois volitans) *is small, elegant, and armed with toxic spines.*
PHOTOGRAPH BY
ANDREA GHISOTTI

Strait of
Gobal

Tiran
Island

Sharm
el-Sheikh

Ras
Mohammad

Shadwan
Island

*Shabrur
Umm Gamar*

Gifatin
Island

Hurghada

Shabrur Umm Gamar

BY ALESSANDRO CARLETTI

Five minutes southwest of Umm Gamar Island by boat, this little reef makes a good dive site for beginners. Boats anchor on the southern side, where the coral wall drops away sheer from a depth of 35 to 50 feet (10 to 15 meters). Swim east, keeping a slight distance from the reef, descending to between 70 and 100 feet (20 to 25 meters). Around the southeastern point, you will see the remains of a wrecked

0 mt
0 ft

10 mt
32 ft

15 mt
50 ft

30 mt
100 ft

modern freighter. Among the cables and the few twisted beams, a spectacular Malabar grouper weighing more than 150 pounds (70 kilograms) often floats along, with its mouth open to allow tiny fish to clean its teeth and gills. It is well accustomed to scuba divers and can be approached easily. Along the reef, beyond a jagged coral wall, you may see gray reef sharks, barracudas, and small groups of jacks.

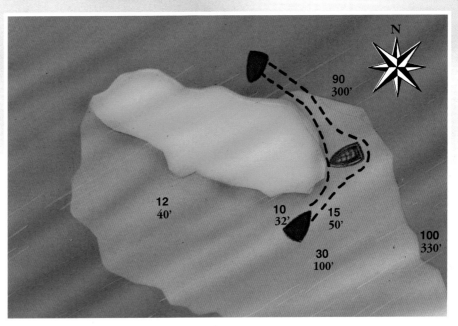

Careless Reef

BY ALESSANDRO
CARLETTI

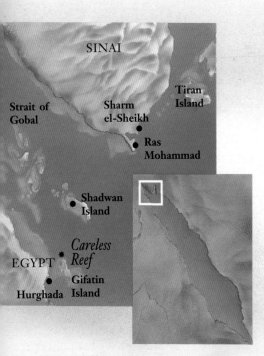

This is the most famous coral reef in the coastal area of Hurghada. It can be reached by boat in about an hour. Careless Reef is made up of a coral ridge extending from east to west, peaking at a depth of 40 to 65 feet (12 to 20 meters). The mooring is near 2 coral towers, each about 100 feet (30 meters) wide, which just break the surface. The seabed, no deeper than 50 to 55 feet (15 to 16 meters) between the towers, drops suddenly 230 feet (60 me-ters) to the east. This sheer wall is dotted with caverns in which glassfish and lionfish live.

The corals are very varied: multicolored soft corals cover the tower walls, and plentiful red fire coral brightens the surface layers. Umbrella acropora, easily the most common, offers shelter to innumerable small coral fish, including anthias, grunts, and angelfish. Gray sharks, whitetip reef sharks, and other pelagic fish can often be seen swimming not

far from the deep cliff. However, moray eels are the main attraction at Careless Reef. You will see them out of their dens, swimming fully extended among the corals. Moray eels keep their fierce-looking mouths open to breath, not to frighten enemies. You should nevertheless respect their menacing appearance and approach them only with a guide, who knows them from experience and may even allow you to pet one in its den.

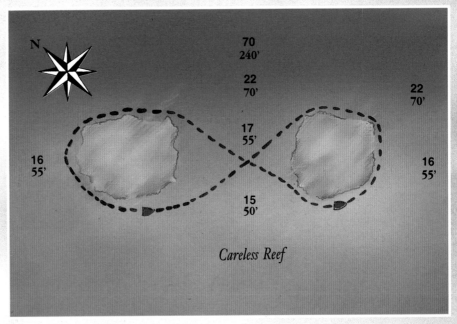

Careless Reef

Giftun Seghir Island

BY ALESSANDRO CARLETTI

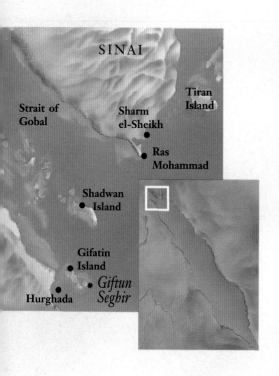

This is the smaller of the two Gifatin Islands at the center of the Hurghada archipelago, half an hour by boat from the town's coast. It is a very demanding dive site, requiring an underwater computer, excellent training, and experience.

The most challenging dive is along the sheer eastern wall, on which black coral, yellow and red sea whip corals, and undulating fans of giant gorgonians thrive in the constant northern current. Boats cannot anchor in the merciless current, so divers must enter the water from a small rocky inlet 160 feet (50 meters) north of the military installation.

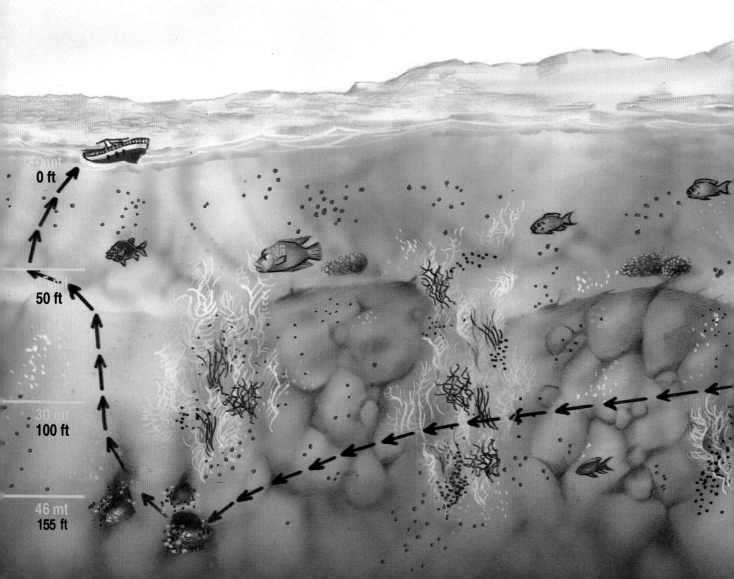

0 ft

50 ft

30 mt
100 ft

46 mt
155 ft

After drifting in the current for about 550 yards (500 meters) at a depth of 100 feet (30 meters), you can swim along another promontory. There, at 150 feet (46 meters), you will find a tunneled-out grotto with double arches, one on top of the other, filled with black coral on a bed of white sand. Swim through the grotto to reach the coral bed at 50 feet (15 meters), and continue westward to the island wall and the lagoon where the dive boat awaits. Tuna, jacks, and plenty of common pelagic fish pass the deep island wall, and many humphead wrasses, coral fish, and moray eels swim in the lagoon.

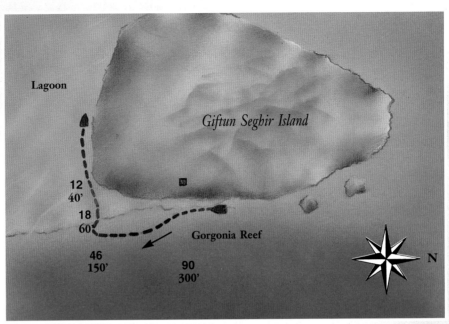

Lagoon

Giftun Seghir Island

12
40'

18
60'

Gorgonia Reef

46
150'

90
300'

N

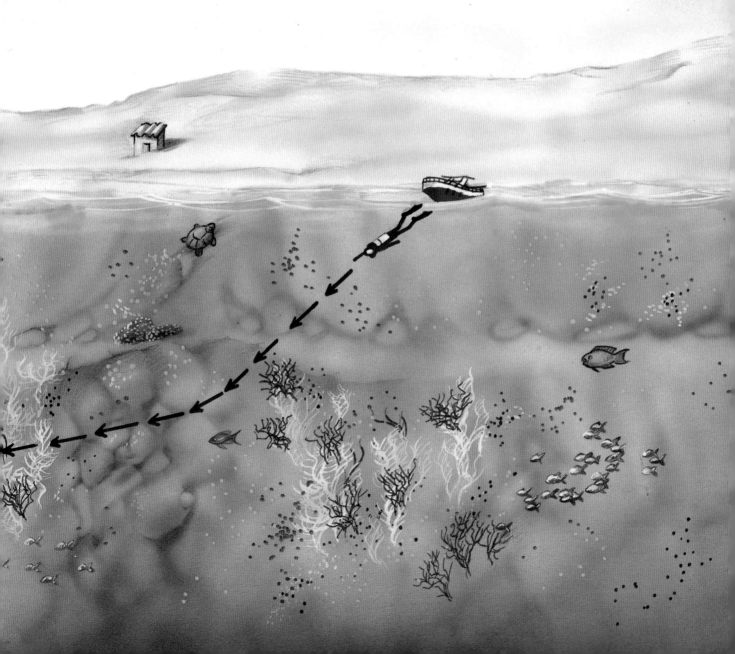

Erg Abu Ramada

BY ALESSANDRO CARLETTI

SINAI

Strait of
Gobal

Tiran
Island

Sharm
el-Sheikh

Ras
Mohammad

Shadwan
Island

Gifatin
Island

Hurghada

*Erg Abu
Ramada*

This small group of reefs breaks the surface 160 feet (50 meters) off the eastern coast of the Abu Ramada Island, 45 minutes by boat from Hurghada. Four small coral towers, two of which break the surface, are set on a bed of rock and coral 56 feet (17 meters) beneath the surface. A fixed mooring is attached to the largest reef. This point, too, is exposed to the powerful currents of the open sea, so coral life abounds, particularly soft corals. The dive route passes among the towers over an area of about 300 feet

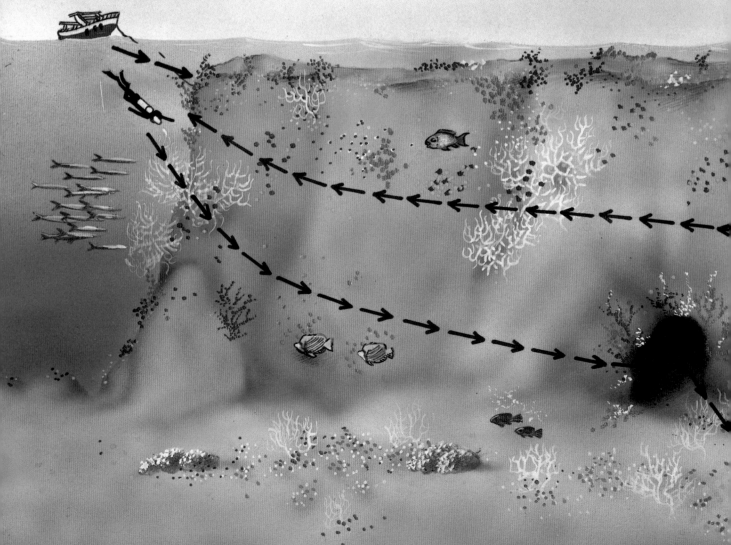

(100 meters), so the current is not a problem to divers.

Erg Abu Ramada is a classic example of the surprising concentration of underwater life at small points in the Red Sea. Red anthias and silvery lunar fusiliers (*Caesio lunaris*) swarm the tops of the reefs, and plenty of groupers swim the seabed. Small orangespotted jacks often hunt the reefs, swimming at great speed among the narrow canyons that separate the coral towers, and you may see small schools of barracuda.

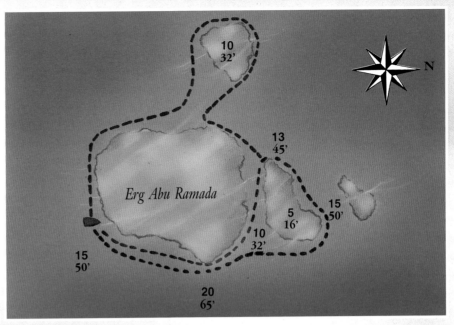

Gota Abu Ramada

BY ALESSANDRO CARLETTI

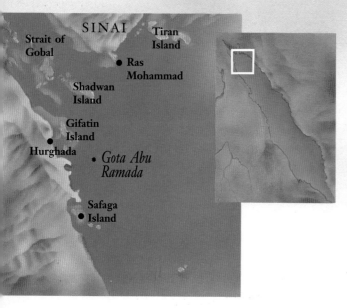

Fifteen minutes by boat south of Abu Ramada, or 45 minutes by boat from Hurghada, brings you to the circular reef of Gota, which just breaks the surface. The reef's perimeter is surrounded by a white seabed of coral sand at a depth of 40 feet (12 meters). Gota may well be the most colorful, luminous, and distinctive tropical reef of Hurghada. The coral shapes are splendid—round, brainlike, or shaped like small umbrellas— and not to be found anywhere

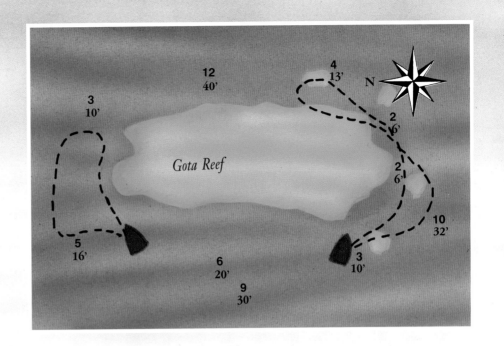

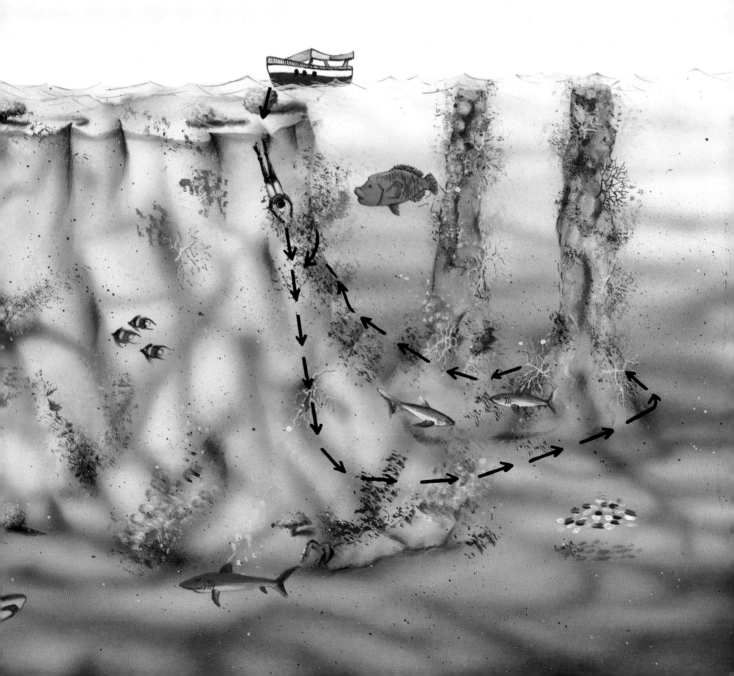

A

B

A. A coral grouper (Cephalopholis miniata) *waits to ambush any unsuspecting small fish. His favorite prey is orange scalefin anthias* (Anthias squamipinnis) *and glassfish.*
PHOTOGRAPH BY
VINCENZO PAOLILLO

B. The waters of the reef of Gota Abu Ramada glitter with the splendid colors of alcyonarians and corals.
PHOTOGRAPH BY
VINCENZO PAOLILLO

C. A school of barracudas (Sphyraena barracuda) *proceeds majestically through the water.*
PHOTOGRAPH BY
ROBERTO RINALDI

else in the archipelago. The wall facing the open sea has the most, and most beautiful, corals. At about 66 feet (20 meters) from the wall, two coral pinnacles glittering with glassfish reach from the seabed to the surface.

Large groups of grunts, butterflyfish, and snappers hover around the reef. Bluespotted lagoon rays rest camouflaged on

C

D

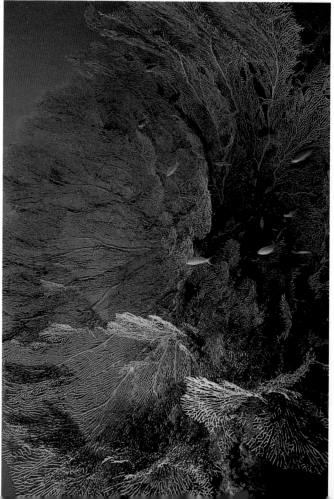

D. Enormous sea fans (Gorgonia ventalina) *reach out to the open sea to filter-feed on plankton.*
PHOTOGRAPH BY
VINCENZO PAOLILLO

the seabed; over them pass gray morays, and sometimes small sharks.

The interior of the reef is less lush, but there are two satellite reefs, full of interesting nooks and crannies. A number of curious turkeyfish live permanently around one of the satellite reefs. These particular turkeyfish feel very comfortable with scuba divers and sometimes like to tease them, swimming tauntingly close, so remember that they have poisonous spines and keep your distance. During the summer you will see male titan triggerfish *(Balistoides viridescens)* intently protecting their nests. Females lay the eggs in broad craters dug into the sand by the males, who then hang vertically upside-down over the nest, blowing powerful jets of water into the sand. Avoid swimming near or above their nests—triggerfish have strong teeth and a powerful bite and are quite aggressive and territorial during nesting periods.

The wide variety of subjects, abundance of color and light, and crystal waters make this a classic dive for photographers.

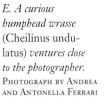

E. A curious humphead wrasse (Cheilinus undulatus) *ventures close to the photographer.*
PHOTOGRAPH BY ANDREA AND ANTONELLA FERRARI

F. The walls of the reef abound with colonies of the tiny alcyonarian polyps.
PHOTOGRAPH BY VINCENZO PAOLILLO

G. The wealth of corals on the reef walls and along the coral pinnacles make Gota Abu Ramada an unrivaled undersea paradise. In this picture, an enormous sea fan and a number of alcyonarians make a natural frame for the image of a saber squirrelfish (Adoryx spinifer).
PHOTOGRAPH BY ALBERTO VANZO

H. A group of snappers (Lutjanus monostigma), *residents of the reef, swim up along the coral wall.*
PHOTOGRAPH BY VINCENZO PAOLILLO

Brother Islands

by Alessandro Carletti

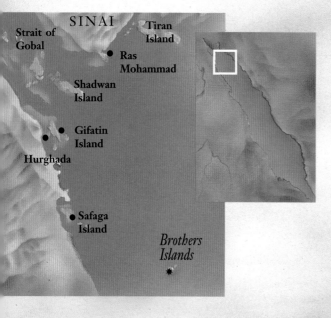

These two small islands, just breaking the surface in the center of the Red Sea and opposite Al Quseir, are the peaks of two pillars surrounded by a narrow coastal reef that drops to 1,000 feet (300 meters). The larger of the two, Big Brother, is about 110 yards (100 meters) across and 440 yards (400 meters) long, with two extremities to the east and west. The smaller island, Little Brother, is round and sits about 875 yards (800 meters) from the big one.

SINAI

Strait of Gobal

Tiran Island

Ras Mohammad

Shadwan Island

Gifatin Island

Hurghada

Safaga Island

Brothers Islands

0 mt
0 ft

30 mt
100 ft

60 mt
200 ft

The two Brothers are the only reefs for dozens of square miles, so many pelagic fish come regularly in search of food. The reefs' exposure to the currents of the open sea has promoted a proliferation of coral—particularly giant gorgonians and soft corals, and especially in the top 100 feet (30 meters) under the surface around Little Brother. This area is worth a full exploration.

Boats cannot anchor safely here—the islands are too small

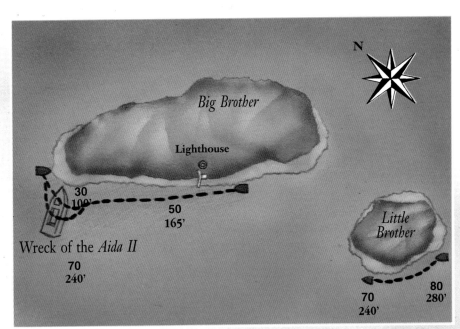

Big Brother

Lighthouse

30
100'

50
165'

Wreck of the *Aida II*

70
240'

Little Brother

70
240'

80
280'

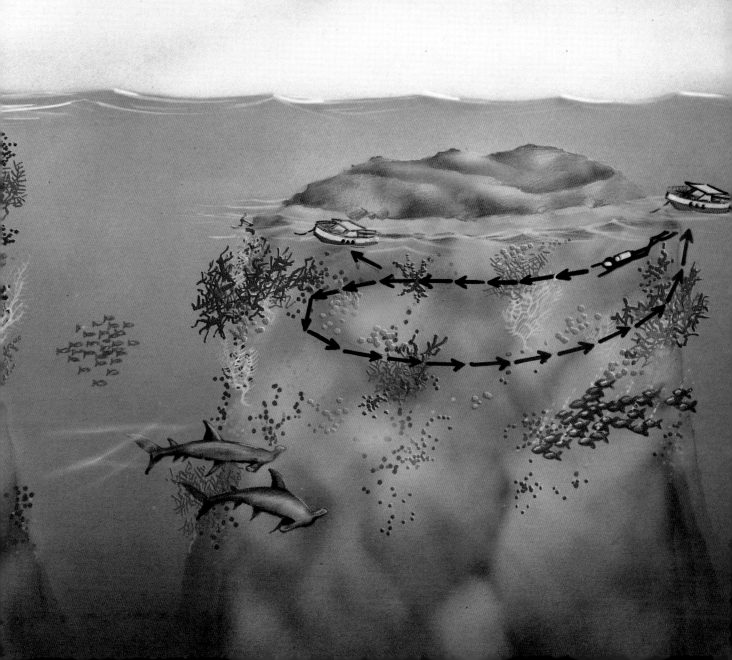

A. The Brother Islands sit at the center of the Red Sea, far away from the usual tourist attractions. Big Brother can easily be recognized by the military lighthouse built by the English in 1880.
PHOTOGRAPH BY MARCELLO BERTINETTI

B. The sometimes menacing whitetip reef shark (Triaenodon obesus) rises from the deepest seabeds. Distinguished by its rounded dorsal fin with a white tip, it grows up to 13 feet (4 meters) in length and is considered dangerous to humans.
PHOTOGRAPH BY ANDREA AND ANTONELLA FERRARI

and the walls too steep. You must take a short cruise (from Hurghada or Port Safaga, for example) and pick a time of year when diving conditions are at their best, usually in May, June, and July.

Big Brother is easily identified by an automatic lighthouse, now tended by Egyptian soldiers,

D. It is not uncommon to encounter sea turtles (Eretmochelys imbricata) during dives off the Brother Islands. This specimen shows no fear of humans.
PHOTOGRAPH BY CARLO DE FABIANIS

C. Little Brother has a unique and spectacular population of gorgonian fans and soft corals.
PHOTOGRAPH BY MARCELLO BERTINETTI

that was built by the English in 1880. Until a few years ago, it still had the marvelous pivoting searchlight devised by the Change Brothers of Birmingham, England.

There is a wreck at the western tip of Big Brother: the *Aida II*, a military craft that went down in 1957 while transporting troops from Alexandria. It had been

E. Large schools of blacktongue unicornfish (Naso hexacanthus) *swim along the reef in the dark nighttime waters in search of food.*
PHOTOGRAPH BY ITAMAR GRINBERG

F. Spectacular specimens of typical reef inhabitants live along the sheer walls.
PHOTOGRAPH BY ANDREA AND ANTONELLA FERRARI

badly anchored and hit the reef during the change of tide; the crew barely made it to safety on the island. Now overgrown with coral, it lies in sailing position, the prow at 100 feet (30 meters) and the stern at 230 feet (70 meters). It is possible to dive into the interior, but take the proper precautions.

The entire wall to the south of the island is an excellent dive site. Schools of barracuda, jacks, amber jacks, snappers, and sharks (sometimes tiger sharks) can be seen in the deep blue waters.

G. A forest of giant gorgonians on the wall of Little Brother.
PHOTOGRAPH BY PIERFRANCO DILENGE

H. An orangestriped triggerfish (Balistapus undulatus) *shows off its brilliant colors. Its sharp teeth and powerful jaws can tackle a tough meal of sea urchins and crustaceans. It can be extremely aggressive, especially when nesting.*
PHOTOGRAPH BY ANDREA AND ANTONELLA FERRARI

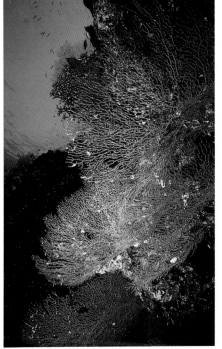

SOUTHERN EGYPT

A

B

Until recently, tourism had long been prohibited in Southern Egypt, so its coasts are the newest addition to a scuba diver's itinerary in the Red Sea. The most interesting dive sites, starting from the north, are Dedalus Reef, 40 miles (65 kilometers) off the coast; the coral system of Fury Shoal, with dozens of reefs of all sizes; the area around Ras Banas, one of the most imposing promontories facing the Red Sea; and the island of Zabargad, with tiny Rocky Island.

Relations with Sudan are still strained, and the entire area is heavily fortified by Egyptian troops. Specific permits are required to sail and moor cruise boats, and the coastline, new to modern tourism, lacks facilities, so local cruises are the only means of arriving at the dive sites. Almost all the boats leave from the small military dock of Ras Qulan, a few miles north of Ras Banas. The best way to get there is by bus from Hurghada, along 250 miles (400 kilometers) of coastal road through the cities of Port Safaga, Al Quseir, and

A. The arid and uninhabited island of Zabargad lies 40 miles southeast of Port Berenice, and rises to a maximum altitude of 492 feet (150 meters).
PHOTOGRAPH BY VINCENZO PAOLILLO

B. The long pier at Dedalus Reef, 40 miles (65 kilometers) from the Egyptian coastline.
PHOTOGRAPH BY VINCENZO PAOLILLO

C. Some ancient Roman amphorae, a few of them intact, have been found in the waters off Dolphin Reef.
PHOTOGRAPH BY PIERFRANCO DILENGE

D. The wreck of a large tugboat on the seabed off Zabargad.
PHOTOGRAPH BY ANDREA GHISOTTI

C

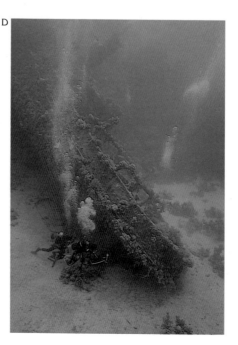

D

Mersa Alam. The cruise boats are all fairly large (minimum 8 passengers), comfortable, and equipped with good navigational gear, which is important given the distance from any tourist facility.

The area's humidity level is high throughout the year, and temperatures can go higher than 104°F (40°C) in the summer. The water temperature remains almost always above 77°F (25°C), but in the summer it can reach 86°F (30°C), triggering a proliferation of plankton that makes visibility a problem. The north wind generates massive seas, and only the larger reefs provide shelter.

The diving is unlimited and the seabeds unspoiled. Corals are less varied than in the northern regions (the Tropic of Capricorn cuts through the Red Sea just a few miles south), and permanent coral fish species are found less on the coastal reefs and more on broad, shallow seabeds, where water circulation is less rapid. Life is plentiful around the outer reefs and the islands, and you will see many large pelagic fish.

E

F

G

H

E. Giant mantas (Manta birostris) *swim elegantly in the seas off southern Egypt.* PHOTOGRAPH BY VINCENZO PAOLILLO

F. Assemblies of scalloped hammerhead sharks (Sphyrna lewini) *are one of the most exciting and moving sights the sea can offer.* PHOTOGRAPH BY BOB CRANSTON/JEFF ROTMAN PHOTOGRAPHY

G. Little bottlenose dolphins (Tursiops truncatus) *swim in the Dolphin Reef.* PHOTOGRAPH BY ANDREA GHISOTTI

H. A gorgonian sea fan, illuminated by the scuba diver's spotlight, reveals the delicate fabric of its branches. PHOTOGRAPH BY VINCENZO PAOLILLO

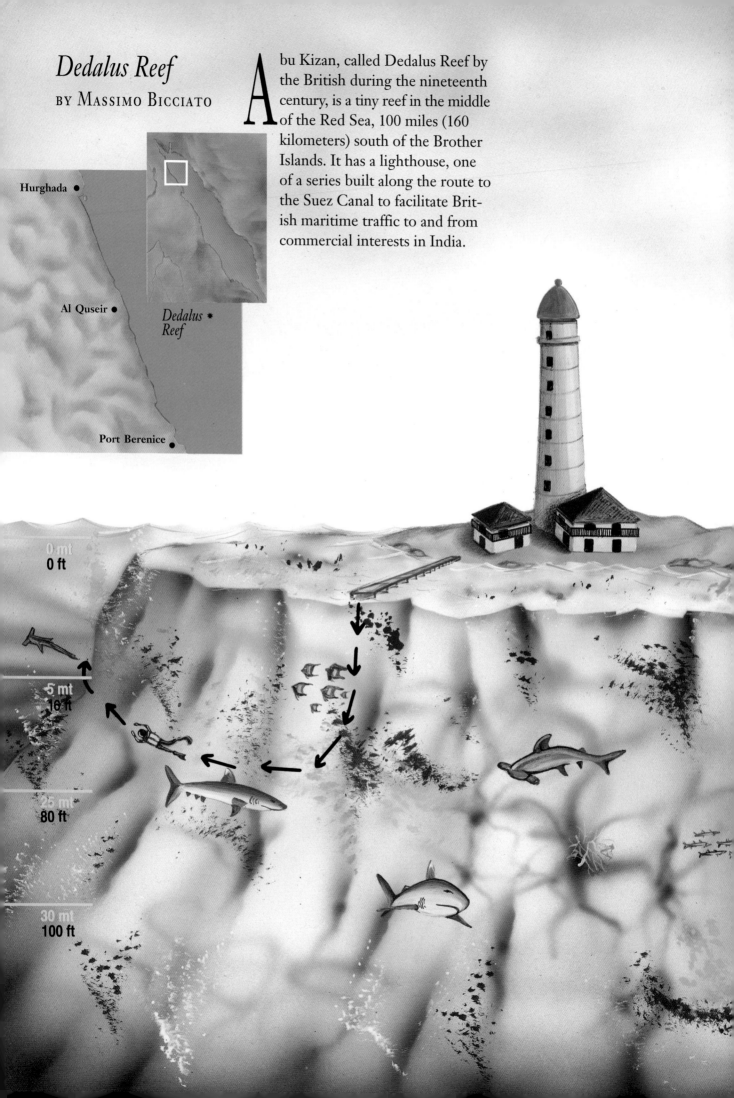

Dedalus Reef
BY MASSIMO BICCIATO

Abu Kizan, called Dedalus Reef by the British during the nineteenth century, is a tiny reef in the middle of the Red Sea, 100 miles (160 kilometers) south of the Brother Islands. It has a lighthouse, one of a series built along the route to the Suez Canal to facilitate British maritime traffic to and from commercial interests in India.

Hurghada

Al Quseir

Dedalus Reef

Port Berenice

0 mt
0 ft

5 mt
16 ft

25 mt
80 ft

30 mt
100 ft

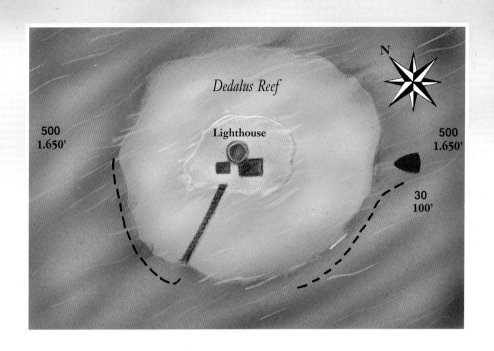

Dedalus Reef

Lighthouse

N

500
1.650'

500
1.650'

30
100'

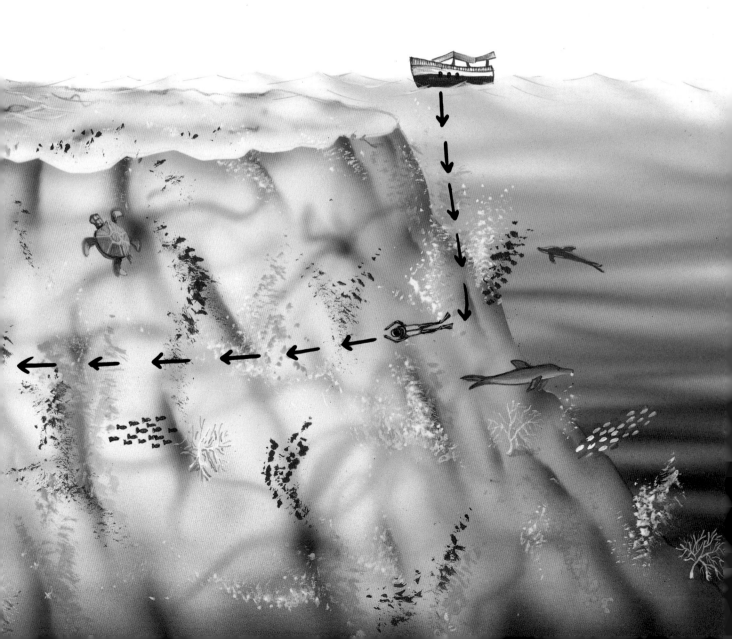

You can get to the lighthouse by walking the wooden ramp that crosses the island's entire width, just 330 feet (100 meters). In the old offices and living quarters, filled with badly worn English furniture and odd objects gathered over time, you are transported to the years of the earliest English steamers, loaded with silks and spices, heading back through the Suez Canal.

A. Dedalus Reef is entirely surrounded by a remarkably beautiful reef that just breaks the surface.
PHOTOGRAPH BY MASSIMO BICCIATO

B. A scuba diver explores the lush walls of Dedalus Reef.
PHOTOGRAPH BY ROBERTO RINALDI

C. Dedalus Reef is almost entirely covered by an automatic lighthouse, of fundamental importance to the safety of shipping.
PHOTOGRAPH BY MASSIMO BICCIATO

The reef's circular perimeter is surrounded by a spectacular reef that just breaks the surface from a depth of over 1,650 feet (500 meters). The sheer walls are teeming with underwater life: the southern wall is covered with white alcyonarians and enormous coral terraces crowded with a multitude of colorful tropical fish. The western wall has a terrace at 82 feet (25 meters) and then drops into the deep. There is an intense population of pelagic life in the deep waters all around the island, including sea turtles, jacks, barracudas, graytip reef sharks, and even hammerhead sharks.

D. *A scuba diver swims undisturbed through a school of twinspot snappers* (Lutjanus bohar).
PHOTOGRAPH BY ROBERTO RINALDI

E. *Silvery twinspot snappers inhabit the coral walls of Dedalus Reef in great numbers.*
PHOTOGRAPH BY CLAUDIO ZIRALDO

F. *Two large bigeye trevallies swim around a branch of alcyonarian.*
PHOTOGRAPH BY MARCO BOSCO

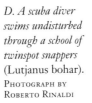

G. *In the waters off Dedalus Reef you can see many passing pelagic fish. Here is a blacktip reef shark accompanied by the inevitable remora, or sharksucker* (Echeneis naucrates).
PHOTOGRAPH BY CLAUDIO ZIRALDO

H. *Rays of sunlight filtering through the sea illuminate a number of multi-colored alcyonarians.*
PHOTOGRAPH BY ROBERTO RINALDI

Dolphin Reef

BY ALESSANDRO CARLETTI

Dolphin Reef

Sha'ab Mahsur

Ras Banas

Port Berenice

Zabargad Island

Rocky Island

Foul Bay

EGYPT

Sataya Reef, widely known as Dolphin Reef, is the largest on the coral ridge of Furey Shoal, a few miles north of Ras Banas. It is almost 2 miles (3 kilometers) long and 195 feet (60 meters) across with a huge sandy lagoon on its southeastern side.

The lagoon is no more than 30 feet (10 meters) deep and permanent home to more than 100 bottlenose dolphins—a few imposing males and a lot of

females with their young. They live peacefully there, but they are unaccustomed to human presence and do not like to be approached too closely.

The northeastern wall descends to 260 feet (80 meters), and then, after a narrow step, disappears into the blue. There is a burst of colorful hard and soft corals in the first several feet under the surface, below which the wall becomes sedimentary,

0 mt
0 ft

10 mt
32 ft

25 mt
80 ft

with some spectacular slides of coral sand.

There are a lot of jacks, amber jacks, and small tuna at this site, and sea turtles often swim on the surface. It is likely that you will see some large predators in the deeper waters, hammerheads and gray sharks in particular. Be aware that, like the dolphins in this area, they are rather touchy and territorial.

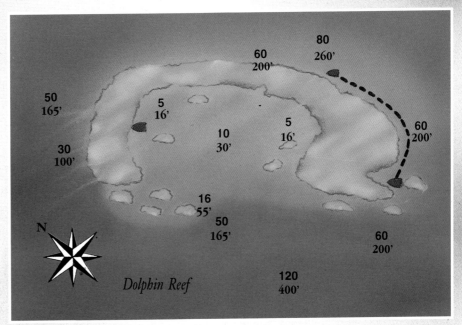

Sha'ab Mahsur

BY ALESSANDRO CARLETTI

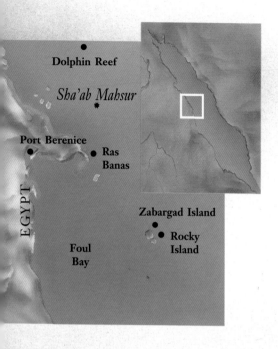

Sha'ab Mahsur is half an hour by boat north of Dolphin Reef. It is much smaller than Dolphin Reef, with long walls to the north and south. The south wall is sheer and its deep ridges teem with coral fish and red and violet soft corals. The red coral has spectacular ocher-colored candelabra with fine white tips. But there is nothing much to see

below 95 feet (30 meters) on either wall.

The two tips of the reef offer the most astonishing, and the deepest, dives. Sea turtles, blacktail sharks, and hammerhead sharks are a frequent sight here. At the tip pointing out to sea there are a few small satellite reefs, one with a lovely grotto passing through it.

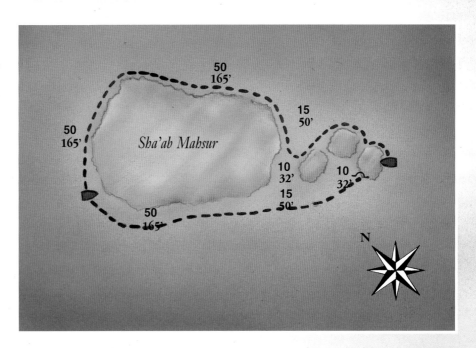

Zabargad Island

BY ALESSANDRO
CARLETTI

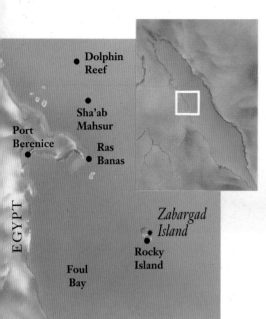

Zabargad, a volcanic island 40 miles (65 kilometers) southeast of Port Berenice, is thought to be the legendary "Topazos" referred to in the *Annales* by Pliny the Elder. Here, pharaohs and Romans mined olivine, a common silicate valuable only when pure and in large pieces. All the finest examples of this precious stone come from Zabargad. It had disappeared from the gem trade for centuries until the Egyptians began to mine it again at the beginning of the twentieth century. Today the island is uninhabited and regularly patrolled by the Egyptian army, due to strained relations with the Sudan.

Across from the old dock, on the great eastern beach, the seabed drops steeply to between 50 and 65 feet (15 to 20 meters). In these waters, dozens of slender coral towers, tastefully decorated with umbrella acropora down the sides and rounded Favites and

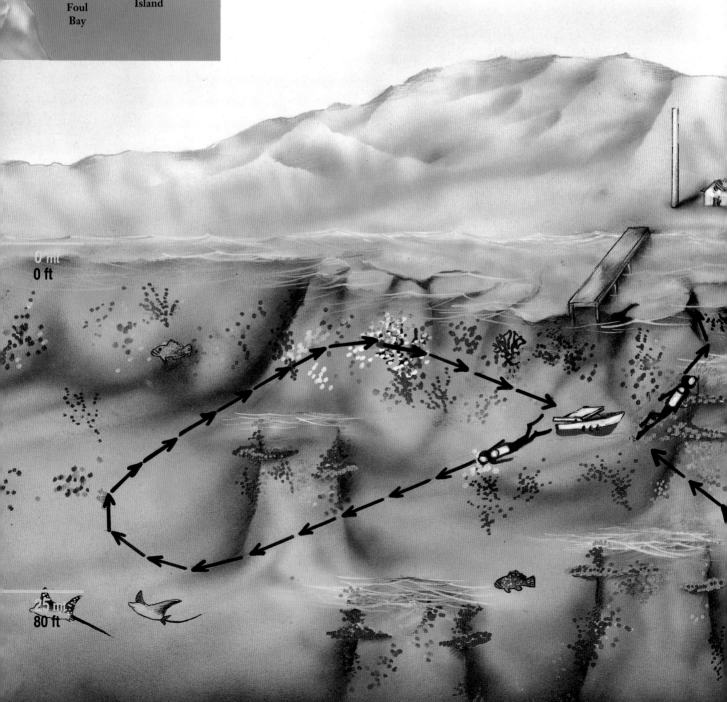

Gonioporae on top, cluster like buildings in a city. In the area immediately around the dock, the tops of the pillars have joined and only a few shafts of light penetrate into the long underwater corridors. Very approachable groupers live here in startling numbers.

This is an amazing dive, especially by night, when octopus, crustaceans, crinoids, and nudibranches crowd the coral grottoes.

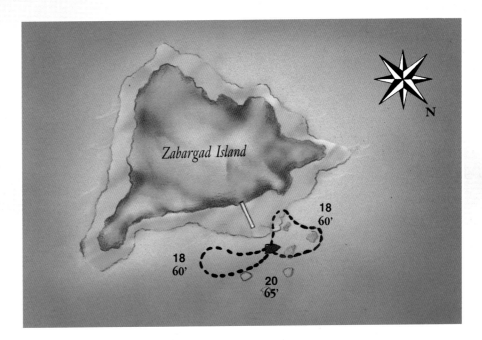

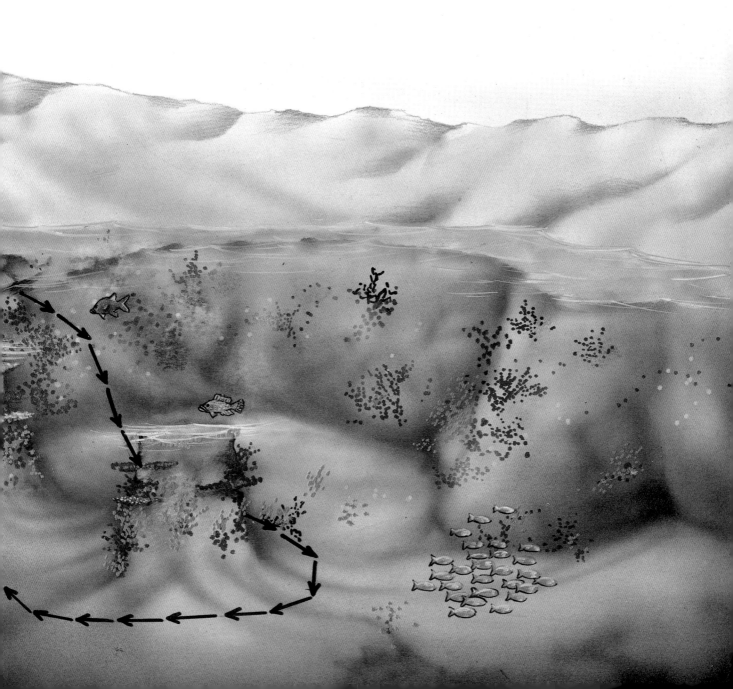

Rocky Island
BY ALESSANDRO CARLETTI

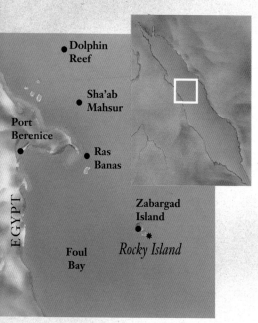

This small, elliptical fossil-coral island, 20 minutes by boat southeast of Zabargad, is surrounded by a surface-level reef several feet wide from which its walls drop more than 3,200 feet (1,000 meters). Cruise ships must keep moving because of the frequent high seas, strong currents, and difficulties in anchoring.

Huge gorgonians, black coral, and soft corals grow in

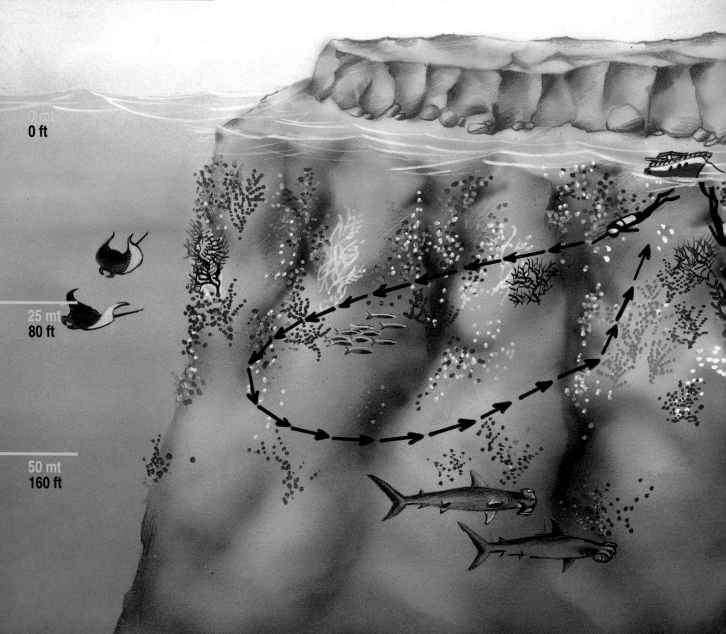

deep canyons in the reef wall. Pelagic fish of all kinds have been seen in the waters around the island, and if you do several short dives over a few days, you will probably see many species of shark. Blacktail sharks are always present, along with barracuda, jacks, eagle rays, manta rays, and tuna. Dives off Rocky Island compare well with those off the Brother Islands, Dedalus Reef, and Ras Mohammad.

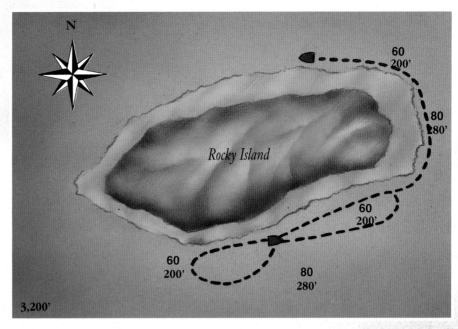

SUDAN

The Sudan has unquestionably one of the most beautiful, complete, and unspoiled seascapes in the world. Although it was the first area of the Red Sea explored by Hans Hass in 1950, and later by Jacques-Yves Cousteau, it still retains its mystery.

A dive trip to the Sudan presents a true adventure—not all of it underwater. The first challenge is trying to get there. Apart from the occasional cruise coming directly from the north, practically all the trips start in Port Sudan, which must be reached by air from Cairo. The flight schedules are absolutely unreliable and you

A. A blacktail shark cruises close to the bottom in the waters off the Sudan, accompanied by a sharksucker.
PHOTOGRAPH BY JACK JACKSON

B. The Sudanese reefs have delicate forests of gorgonian fans.
PHOTOGRAPH BY GIANFRANCO D'AMATO

C. Pretty red sea whips, undulating in the current, brighten deep waters.
PHOTOGRAPH BY ANDREA GHISOTTI

can be stuck for up to two days in Port Sudan, especially on the return trip. (Pilgrims to Mecca take connecting flights to Jedda in Port Sudan, and they are always given precedence.) Many more tourists would come here if this annoying problem were solved.

Scuba divers, having arrived, must be adaptable and have patience. It is difficult for charter boats, which are almost all Italian, to offer any real comfort; each piece of equipment must be brought from Europe. The climate is extremely warm, the port facilities poor, supplies difficult to get, and spare parts almost nonexistent. Still, the overall standard of living on board is sufficient to enjoy the beauties of the sea.

There are two classic itineraries, one to the north and the other to the southeast. Each one usually begins with a wreck dive onto the *Umbria*, which is just out of port. The northern trip continues toward Sanganeb and Sha'ab Rumi. You can go all the way to Sha'ab Su'adi or Angarosh, but this depends on the ocean conditions and requires a lot of time spent sailing. The southern trip involves exploring reefs and islets in the Suakin group, spending the night at Sha'ab Anber, and making daily excursions to the various dive sites nearby. This route requires calm sea and wind, rare conditions in this area, most likely to occur in March. You can take a side trip to Suakin, the ancient "Venice of the Red Sea," long since fallen into total ruin, but make sure you have the right permits.

The climate is warm all year round, but swelters in the summer. The best time for a visit is spring and fall, when the temperature is milder. Ironically, visibility is best and sightings of rare sea creatures more common in the summer, but do not expect to get any sleep in your hot cabin. Water temperature stays around 79 to 85°F (26 to 28°C) in the spring, drops a few degrees in winter, and gets even hotter in the summer.

Charter boats usually offer Italian 15-liter tanks, featuring double valves and weights. Make certain that you bring any other necessary equipment. Film, accessories, batteries, and other supplies are not available locally. Each boat has a generator and an inverter for recharging strobes and lights.

No particular vaccinations are required, but if you need any medicine, make sure you bring a complete supply—local health facilities are poorly stocked. Above all, dive with great caution. There is no help available for divers with the bends or an embolism.

D. A graceful soft coral grows on the sheer reef wall.
PHOTOGRAPH BY ANDREA GHISOTTI

E. A gaudy grouper complements the varied colors of the reef.
PHOTOGRAPH BY CLAUDIO ZIRALDO

G

F

H

F. The wreck of the Blue Bell on the seabed of Sha'ab Su'adi.
PHOTOGRAPH BY ANDREA GHISOTTI

G. Sha'ab Rumi offers one of the most complete dives in the southern Red Sea.
PHOTOGRAPH BY ANDREA GHISOTTI

H. The long wooden pier that leads to the Sanganeb lighthouse.
PHOTOGRAPH BY ANDREA GHISOTTI

Angarosh

BY CLAUDIO CANGINI

*A*ngarosh means "mother of the sharks" in Arabic. This is the most famous dive site on earth for sightings of large predators, from graytip reef sharks (*Carcharhinus amblyrhynchos* and *Carcharhinus albimarginatus*) to the terrible and solitary whitetip reef sharks *(Triaenodon obesus)* to great gatherings of hammerheads *(Sphyrna lewini)* parading through the depths. The pinnacle of Angarosh drops to nearly 2,893 feet (800 meters). Because of the great depth and the constant strong currents, this dive is recommended only for those divers with great ability and experience.

Divers enter the water on the east side of the reef, descending almost vertically to the first terrace at 82 feet (25 meters). A dense school of barracudas swims here among red sea whips and huge multicolored alcyonarians. Swim to the edge of the terrace for a breathtaking look down into the abyss; you will probably see

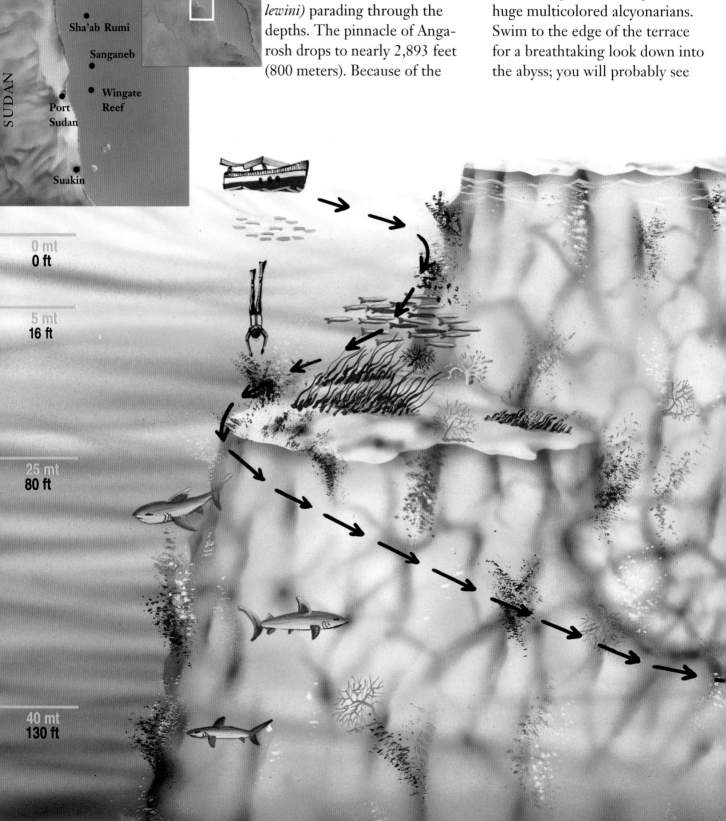

SUDAN

Angarosh

Sha'ab Su'adi

Sha'ab Rumi

Sanganeb

Wingate Reef

Port Sudan

Suakin

0 mt
0 ft

5 mt
16 ft

25 mt
80 ft

40 mt
130 ft

some graytip reef sharks among other passing fish. Cross diagonally down to 130 feet (40 meters) to the second terrace, which is also ablaze with colorful alcyonarians. The most thrilling part of this dive is when you see the dense gatherings of hammerhead sharks, moving through the water together in groups of 30 or 40. Swim up and along the west side of the pinnacle to the support inflatable.

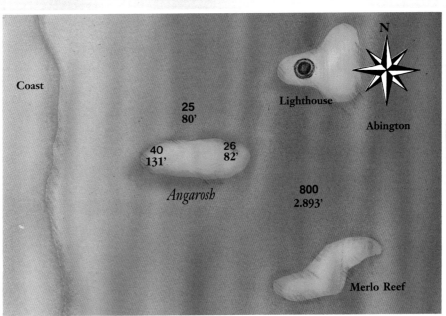

Sha'ab Su'adi: Wreck of the Blue Bell

BY ANDREA GHISOTTI

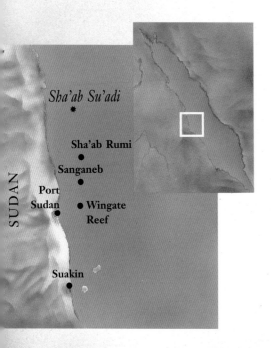

Mersa Arakiyai (*mersa* means "sheltered bay") is about 40 miles (65 kilometers) north of Port Sudan. Just off the coast here is Sha'ab Su'adi, a reef easily identified by masses of metallic wreckage—the remains of a few automobiles from the wreck of the *Blue Bell*. In the late 1970s, this large cargo ship inexplicably struck the reef, damaged its keel, and sank to the bottom. It overturned on the scarp, prow toward the reef, 260 feet (80 meters) under. Its cargo of Toyota vehicles—four-doors, pickups, large trucks, and panel vans—now lies tangled in the wreck or scattered along the seabed.

0 mt
0 ft

55 mt
180 ft

80 mt
280 ft

This dive is memorable for the clarity of the water and the amazing setting for the passing pelagic fish provided by the huge wreck and its cargo. Midway along the ship, the scarp drops sharply to about 180 feet (55 meters), leaving a gap between the bottom and the hull of the ship, where the current nourishes some unusually large soft corals. The bridge, the screw, and the rudder are still intact at 230 feet (70 meters), too deep for a thorough exploration.

Dangerous mako sharks and tiger sharks emerge at night from the depths, so night dives to this wreck are not recommended.

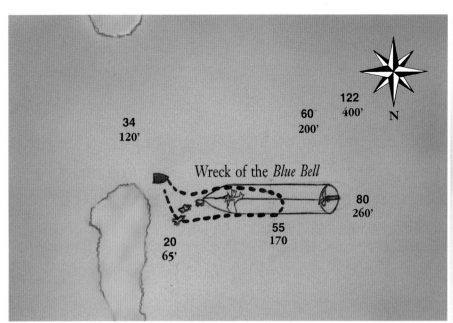

Wreck of the *Blue Bell*

34
120'

122
400'

60
200'

80
260'

20
65'

55
170

N

Sha'ab Rumi: South Point

BY ANDREA GHISOTTI

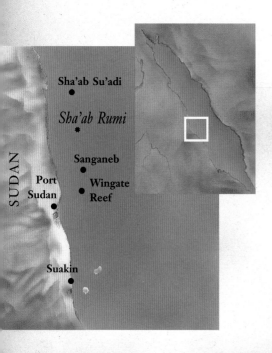

Sha'ab Su'adi

Sha'ab Rumi

Sanganeb

Port
Sudan

Wingate
Reef

SUDAN

Suakin

Sha'ab Rumi, 25 miles from Port Sudan, is one of the underwater wonders of the world—it certainly offers one of the most complete dives in these waters. The clarity of the water is as startling as its wealth of fish. It was here in 1963 that Jacques-Yves Cousteau organized *Precontinent II*, the huge experiment in underwater living.

You can take shelter from the rough seas on the interior of the lagoon, accessible through a pass on the west side. From here, the

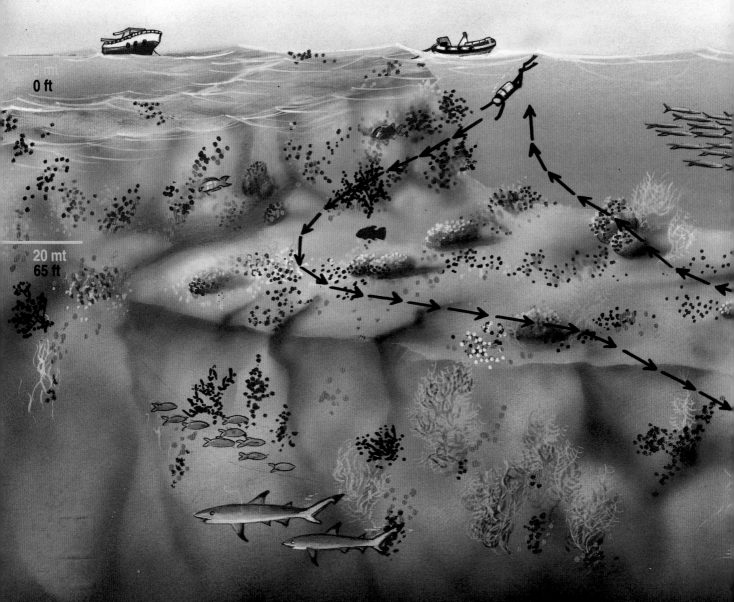

0 ft

20 mt
65 ft

South Point is a short trip by dinghy; leave the boat in the lagoon. (The sandy lagoon itself makes a great night dive.) The point is often subject to strong currents that sweep in a number of directions, but generally southwesterly.

There is a huge shallow pool (too shallow for divers) just off the coast with beautiful corals growing in the first few inches under the surface. A number of fish species have chosen this pool as a nursery, and their young

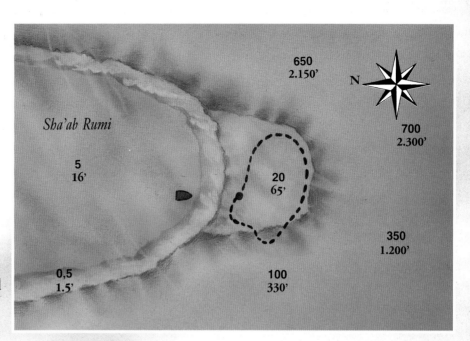

Sha'ab Rumi

650
2.150'

700
2.300'

5
16'

20
65'

350
1.200'

0,5
1.5'

100
330'

gradually falling away. The other sides drop away sharply to depths of over 2,300 feet (700 meters). These walls are upholstered with small gorgonians and soft corals of every color, and nearly every species of reef fish in the Red Sea can be spotted here. There is an endless procession of pelagic fish, which approach divers fearlessly, making for wonderful photo-

A. A school of goatfish (Mulloides vanicolensis) swims in close formation along the rocks. This diurnal fish lives in groups of 200, often moving along sandy seabeds or at the base of a reef. They monitor their territory for mollusks and other small prey with the long barbels just beneath their mouths.
PHOTOGRAPH BY VINCENZO PAOLILLO

grow here in the peaceful presence of surgeonfish.

The most distinctive feature of South Point is the platform that surrounds it like a huge diving board into the inaccessible depths. The wall of the point facing the open sea drops straight to 80 feet (20 meters) and then continues gently southward for another 330 feet (100 meters),

B. Hammerhead sharks are a common sight off the South Point of Sha'ab Rumi. These much feared predators move in schools of 20 to 30 individuals. They are actually quite shy and avoid scuba divers.
PHOTOGRAPH BY ANDREA GHISOTTI

C. A parrotfish is accompanied by a single butterflyfish while it makes the rounds on a rocky seabed.
PHOTOGRAPH BY ANDREA AND ANTONELLA FERRARI

D. Silvery barracudas are a frequent presence off South Point.
PHOTOGRAPH BY DUBA

graphs. Dense schools of barracuda move about, tending to congregate along the eastern ridge, and sharks abound: whitetip reef sharks, graytip sharks, and especially hammerheads. The hammerheads go out on patrol together in the deeper waters along the platform and then disappear out to sea. Sometimes you can see groups of 20 to 30 hammerheads, some of them very

E. A coral grouper moves freely along the intricate forms of the reef. This typical coral fish is about 16 inches (40 centimeters) long and lives at depths ranging from 6.5 to 328 feet (2 to 100 meters).
Photograph by Andrea and Antonella Ferrari

large. These fearful predators are quite timid and move off when they are followed, so the best tactic is to float motionless at a depth of at least 100 feet (30 meters).

A typical dive at South Point involves a circumnavigation of the shelf, with brief excursions into deeper water, reaching the deepest areas in the first part of the dive. Then draw back onto the shelf, which rises from 65 feet (20 meters) at the end of the dive. Relax for a while near the surface, and enjoy the rich and colorful waters. Be warned—an occasional gray shark, crisscrossing the shelf nervously, may disturb you.

F. The squirrelfish is easily identified by its large eyes and garish red coloring. This is a typically nocturnal fish, searching for food at night, but hiding in cavities in the reef during the day.
Photograph by Vincenzo Paolillo

G. A group of scuba divers swims around a giant coral umbrella.
Photograph by Andrea Ghisotti

H. Beautiful soft corals can be found in shallow Sudanese waters.
Photograph by Vincenzo Paolillo

Sha'ab Rumi: Remains of Precontinent II

BY ANDREA GHISOTTI

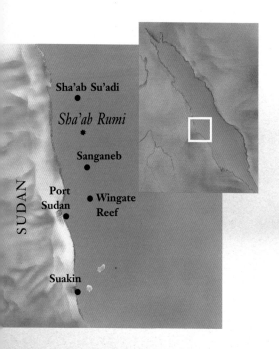

A handsome lagoon opens out on the interior of Sha'ab Rumi. It can be reached through a narrow pass from which you are almost certain to see dolphins cheerfully greeting the boats that come close to shore. Just outside the pass lie the remains of one of Cousteau's most famous expeditions, *Precontinent II*, which was mounted in 1963. This was the first time that divers attempted to make long-term underwater stays in specially built "villages."

A dive to these remains evokes nostalgia for the magic created by

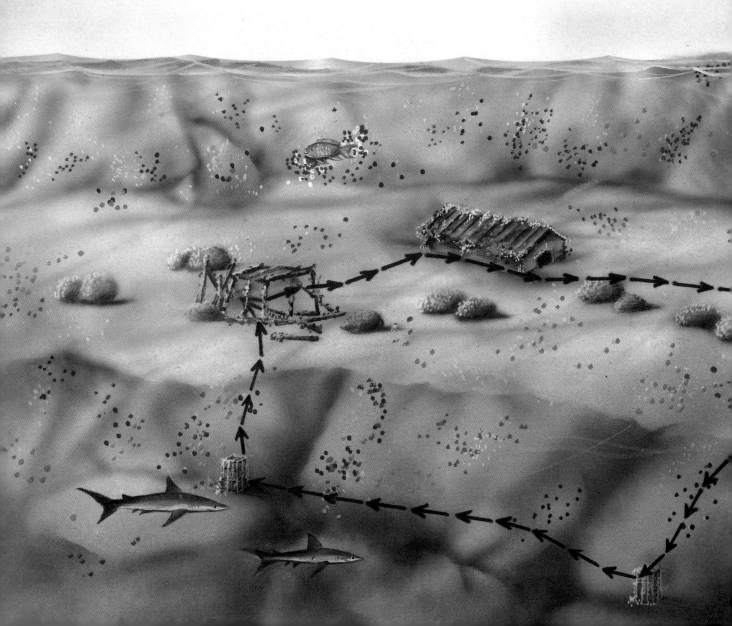

Cousteau, and awe at what he accomplished over 30 years ago in open Red Sea waters. The structures, which would be a challenge to assemble even today, were designed and built on the Côte d'Azur and transported here by the Italian support ship *Rosaldo*. The main structure was star-shaped and served as lodgings for the "oceanauts." Unfortunately, it was recovered at the end of the mission and is absent. The circular garage for the *Soucoupe Plongéante*, the research submarine used for deep

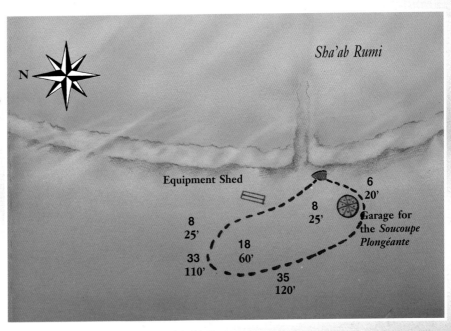

A. The garage for the Soucoupe Plongéante, *part of Jacques Cousteau's 1963 underwater project* Preconti-nent II. *This project was an investigation into whether divers could live under-water for an entire month.*
PHOTOGRAPH BY
ANDREA GHISOTTI

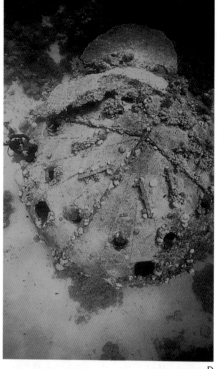

B. *The shape of the garage for the Sou-coupe Plongéante was clearly inspired by the skeleton of a sea urchin. The sheet metal is now encrusted with some very large corals.*
PHOTOGRAPH BY
ANDREA GHISOTTI

explorations, resembles the exo-skeleton of a giant sea urchin and is the most impressive of the abandoned structures. It looks like a huge overturned bowl anchored to the bottom and equipped with a series of circular windows. The lively yellow paint has long since faded, and a num-ber of small madrepores of vari-ous species have attached to the metal. A giant coral umbrella shades the garage, sometimes shelter for a handsome grouper. You can easily explore inside, where you will find a colony of glassfish (who love even the gloomiest of wrecks). The high part has no portholes and is still hermetically sealed. Numerous scuba divers have left behind an air bubble and you can actually

C. *Multicolored encrustations of hard and soft coral cover the abandoned structures of* Precontinent II.
PHOTOGRAPH BY
ANDREA GHISOTTI

D. *A scuba diver observes the few remains of the equipment shed. The underwater village was the set for Cousteau's film* Le Monde sans soleil *(The world without sun).*
PHOTOGRAPH BY
ANDREA GHISOTTI

E

F

G

H

I

E. A lunartail grouper (Variola louti) *swims just above the seabed, wary of the scuba diver.*
Photograph by DUBA

F. The zebra shark (Stegostoma fasciatum) *can grow to as long as 10 feet (3 meters), but is not considered dangerous to humans. It lives chiefly near coral reefs and sandy areas at moderate depths.*
Photograph by Andrea and Antonella Ferrari

G. The coloring of the emperor angelfish (Pomacanthus imperator) *is among the most spectacular, alternating from dark blue to bright yellow and from white to purple.*
Photograph by Marcello Bertinetti

H. A bluespotted stingray lies flat on the sea floor, partially covered with sand.
Photograph by Andrea Ghisotti

I. Life continues around the remains of Cousteau's village. Here, a giant moray curiously emerges from its grotto.
Photograph by DUBA

emerge, remove your mask and regulator, and have a short conversation with your buddy to try out the bizarre echo. The equipment shed is still nearby, and a little farther on, you can glimpse the remains of the fish corral, where fish were penned in for experiments, unforgettably documented in *Le Monde sans soleil* (The world without sun). The garage has been transformed into a beautiful edifice by a stunning coat of sponges and soft corals, around which you may spot a graceful lionfish or a bluespotted stingray. The shark cages are farther down, also transformed by splendid sponges and coral encrustations.

What you won't see are the enormous quantities of fish that appear in the 1960s film. Before shooting began for *Precontinent II*, the area was planted continually for over a month, creating a sort of man-made oasis to attract creatures. Today there is no serious lack of fish, but no guarantee of seeing sharks and jacks on every dive.

Sanganeb

BY ANDREA GHISOTTI

This is the first real reef you see when heading northeast from Port Sudan. Unlike Wingate Reef, famous for the wreck of the *Umbria*, it stands in the open sea, separated from the coast by seabeds that reach depths of 2,600 feet (800 meters). It is the means of access to the canal that leads to Port Sudan and so has a tall lighthouse cemented onto its

0 mt
0 ft

20 mt
65 ft

40 mt
140 ft

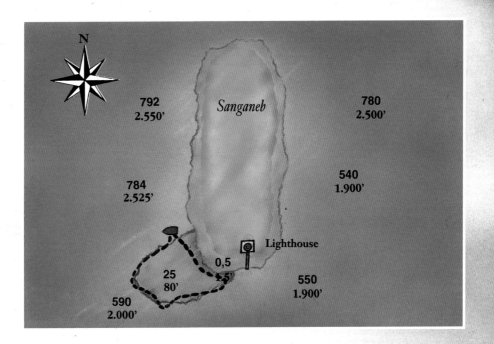

southern surface. Three watch-men stay on the island for days at a time to tend the lighthouse, and they are delighted to exchange a few words with tourists and to show anyone interested the sensational view from the lantern.

The lighthouse is linked to the water by a long catwalk, which rests directly on the partially submerged reef. Surgeonfish live there peacefully, disturbed only by the occasional moray eel or fish hawk. This remarkable range of shallows, only a few inches deep, ends suddenly toward the south, where the outer wall drops straight down into the blue. The wall is thoroughly carpeted in soft corals and is swarming with fish; groupers and grunts, in families of up to 100 individuals, throng its many grottoes. In fact, it is so photogenic that some charter boats spend their entire cruise here.

To the west, there is a saddle that joins the vertical wall to a sandy shelf at about 65 feet (20 meters). The coral sand on the bottom makes the setting very bright, perfect for underwater photography. The many creatures have become accustomed to scuba divers, who often

A

B

A. The platform before the lighthouse of Sanganeb, set in the splendid, emerald-green reef.
PHOTOGRAPH BY
ANDREA GHISOTTI

B. The lighthouse is connected to the water by a very long catwalk.
PHOTOGRAPH BY
ANDREA GHISOTTI

C

D

C. The walls of Sanganeb's reefs are extremely rich in life. The fish are now quite accustomed to scuba divers and allow them to approach without fear. In this picture, a yellowspotted burrfish (Chilomycterus spilostylus) *takes on its typical defensive position with its spines erect, but does not flee from the diver.*
PHOTOGRAPH BY
ANDREA GHISOTTI

D. A scuba diver admires the sinuous branches of sea whip corals swaying in the current.
PHOTOGRAPH BY
ANDREA GHISOTTI

feed the fish to get good photographs. There is always a large school of barracuda that float in the water and can be approached without difficulty, and large parrot fish shuttle between the surface and the sea floor. A few coral pinnacles (thick with gorgonians, soft corals, sponges, black coral, mollusks, and bryonzoans) give shelter to a multitude of crustaceans and small coral fish. They are also cruised by a constant procession of gray sharks, who come fearlessly close to scuba divers. In deeper waters, to the south and southwest, hammerheads swim in large groups, sometimes coming close enough to be photographed. Many blue-spotted stingrays root around on the sandy bottom for small crustaceans and fish. There are always dense schools of silvery jacks, and from time to time you may spot a manta ray or a sea turtle. Photographers should look out for the sea whips, which look dark brown to the eye, but brighten to a pretty red when shot with an electronic strobe.

E. A blacktail shark gives the photographer a glimpse of its white belly as it turns.
PHOTOGRAPH BY PIERFRANCO DILENGE

F. The imposing silhouette of a hammerhead against the blue water.
PHOTOGRAPH BY ANDREA GHISOTTI

G. Soft coral formations cover the reef walls with dense growth here.
PHOTOGRAPH BY ANDREA GHISOTTI

H. Many fish shelter in the labyrinth of the reef wall. Here, a grouper examines a diver from the safety of its den.
PHOTOGRAPH BY VINCENZO PAOLILLO

I. A titan triggerfish (Balistoides viridiscens) moves across the reef, keeping an eye on its territory.
PHOTOGRAPH BY GIANNI LUPARIA

Wingate Reef: Wreck of the Umbria

BY ANDREA GHISOTTI

Ever since the first exploration by the Austrian pioneer Hans Hass in 1950, the wreck of the *Umbria* has been an almost mandatory destination for scuba divers visiting the Sudan. It is, in fact, one of the most famous sunken ships in the world. Built in Hamburg in 1912 and christened the *Bahia Blanca*, the ship was later purchased by the Compagnia Italia, rechristened the *Umbria*, and sold to Lloyd's Triestino in 1937. The huge freighter, 500 feet (150 meters) long with a displacement of 10,000 tons, was driven by two engines with a horsepower of 4,600. Her story is bloodless, even though she sank

0 ft

140 ft

during wartime in 1940, just a few hours before Italy officially entered the war.

The *Umbria*'s last task was to carry war material to the Italian troops in East Africa: sacks of cement, automobiles, and 360,000 bombs, in addition to a ship's usual cargo. The British, aware and covetous of the ship's cargo, engineered bureaucratic delays to keep the *Umbria* in Wingate Reef, where they could examine it thoroughly. There it remained until June 9, 1940. Captain Muiesan discovered through a radio news report that hostilities would begin at midnight. He secretly gave orders to

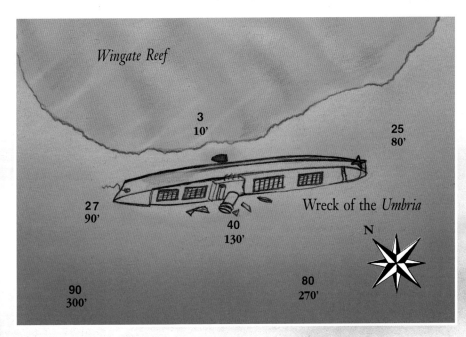

Wingate Reef

3
10'

25
80'

27
90'

40
130'

Wreck of the *Umbria*

N

90
300'

80
270'

A. The large stern of the wreck of the Umbria, *one of the most famous sunken ships in the world.*
PHOTOGRAPH BY ANDREA GHISOTTI

B. The Umbria's *narrow prow sprawls on the seabed.*
PHOTOGRAPH BY ANDREA GHISOTTI

C. *Abundant coral encrustations have taken over the great starboard screw.*
PHOTOGRAPH BY ANDREA GHISOTTI

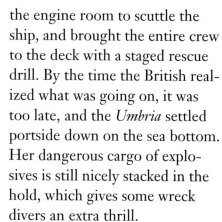

the engine room to scuttle the ship, and brought the entire crew to the deck with a staged rescue drill. By the time the British realized what was going on, it was too late, and the *Umbria* settled portside down on the sea bottom. Her dangerous cargo of explosives is still nicely stacked in the hold, which gives some wreck divers an extra thrill.

The waters are relatively shallow, ranging from several feet to

D. *The starboard gantries break the surface at the center of the ship.*
PHOTOGRAPH BY ANDREA GHISOTTI

a maximum of 130 feet (40 meters), so it is possible to tour the wreck in just one dive. In fact, the spectacular central quarter-deck, with the remains of the huge smokestack, can be dived without tanks. Divers generally start with the ship's midsection, where the starboard gantries of the lifeboats emerge from the water. Some large and friendly triggerfish live around the various decks, and will take morsels of food right from your hand. If you drop to the sea floor here, at a depth of 130 feet (40 meters) you can see

E. In one of her side holds, the Umbria was carrying three Fiat 1100 automobiles, designed specifically for the colonies in East Africa.
PHOTOGRAPH BY ANDREA GHISOTTI

the lifeboats, a giant wind sleeve, and the smokestack. Swim toward the stern to see the holds, where the bombs are stacked with the fuses and other material. The extreme stern is very impressive, with the huge rudder and enormous and heavily encrusted starboard screw. Swim back to the midsection and explore the bow holds; in the first hold, in front of the quarter-deck, are three Fiat 1100 Lunga automobiles in the colonial version, with distinctive treads and three rows of seats. The forward holds contain lots of material: cement sacks, bottles of wine, zippers, lightbulbs, airplane tires, and perfume essences.

F. A considerable portion of the cargo consisted of war materials destined for Italian troops in East Africa. Here are some of the bombs, still neatly stacked in the hold.
PHOTOGRAPH BY ANDREA GHISOTTI

G. The Umbria has become a permanent home for many fish. Here is a brightly colored angelfish.
PHOTOGRAPH BY ANDREA AND ANTONELLA FERRARI

H. A parrotfish swims through the twisted girders of the wreck.
PHOTOGRAPH BY DUBA

ERITREA
Dahlak Islands

A. Angelfish tend to lead solitary lives, moving through protected lagoons or in the shelter of the coral reef.
PHOTOGRAPH BY
ANDREA GHISOTTI

B. Bluestriped snappers usually move in dense schools of more than 1,000 fish. The schools break up into smaller groups at night, when the fish hunt crustaceans on the reef.
PHOTOGRAPH BY
CLAUDIO ZIRALDO

Eritrea reopened its doors to tourism after the popular referendum in 1993, but it still has organizational problems linked to the precarious state of the nation after many years of war with Ethiopia. Diving facilities are only just beginning to emerge, and visitors to the Dahlak Islands must be adaptable. Use the local sailing vessels, which are simple but extremely reliable, in the absence of well-equipped charter cruises.

The point of departure for the Dahlak Islands is the port of Massawa, which is 80 miles (130 kilometers) from Asmara by road. There are a number of hotels in Massawa, all damaged by the war but under reconstruction. All divers must get a fishing permit,

C. Manta rays live around the Dahlak Islands in great numbers, often coming close to shore. There are some enormous specimens, with wingspans of up to 20 feet (6 meters), in these waters.
PHOTOGRAPH BY
VINCENZO PAOLILLO

issued at the port, and must be accompanied by a local guide.

The archipelago is made up of 126 islands with a coral base (although Dissei and Seil are rather rocky), on a sandy seabed that varies in depth from 160 to 330 feet (50 to 100 meters). This rather shallow shelf with a sandy bottom can reduce visibility, and the waters are exceptionally rich

D. A large member of the Haemulidae family has allowed the photographer to come very close, and displays no fear whatsoever. These fish, quite numerous off the Dahlak Islands, are distinguished by their protruding lips.
PHOTOGRAPH BY
ANDREA GHISOTTI

in plankton, which further reduces visibility. Sheer cliffs with deep fissures are quite rare, and at their highest are only several yards high. There are no major coral constructions and none of the classic surface reefs.

There is, however, a remarkable wealth of fish, helped by enforced protection during the war. Some very large groupers, grunts, and snappers have never seen humans and allow divers to approach freely. Mantas and eagle rays come close to the shore and can be seen in large groups at certain times of the year. Sea turtles are very common, emerging by night to lay eggs in the sand. These waters were once considered to be the most shark-infested in the Red Sea, and sharks are in relative plenty, although you won't see any more than you did in the Sudan unless you fish while you dive.

Choose the time of year to come here carefully. It is dark and rainy in the winter, and Massawa is one of the hottest cities on earth during the summer. The best water conditions occur during April and May and in October and early November.

E. Many sharks live in the southern Red Sea; this is a blacktail (Carcharhinus wheeleri). *They seldom show any hostility and prefer to stay at a distance from scuba divers.*
PHOTOGRAPH BY
ANDREA GHISOTTI

F. Seil, a small rocky island in the Dahlak archipelago, is the main nesting site for a great many birds, including herons, storks, spoonbills, seagulls, pelicans, and terns.
PHOTOGRAPH BY
ANDREA GHISOTTI

G. An exhausted sea turtle returns to the water after laying her eggs on the beach during the night.
PHOTOGRAPH BY
ANDREA GHISOTTI

Difnein Island

BY ANDREA GHISOTTI

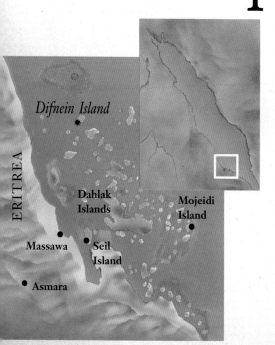

This is the northernmost and most popular of the Dahlak Islands. It is uninhabited and rather isolated, 70 miles (113 kilometers) from Massawa. In the 1970s, before the outbreak of war blocked access, most people came here to hunt the lush underwater life. The seabeds can be explored once again, but the beautiful white beaches are now scattered with mines (at least one fisherman has lost a foot by stepping on one of them), so you cannot get a close look at the island's many varieties of birds and animals.

The water off Difnein is the cleanest of any of the Dahlak Islands, because of its location at the northernmost limit of the archipelago's sandy bottom. The seabeds around the island are about 200 or 230 feet (60 to 70 meters) deep, but a couple of miles east of the island they reach to almost 1,000 feet (300 meters). The northeastern side is the most interesting, though none of it is as spectacular as other Red Sea dive sites. There is a small coral cliff about 16 to 20 feet (5 to 6 meters) high that ends in the sandy bottom at about 50 feet (15 meters). There

0 ft

50 ft

are many fish, so in just one dive you will probably see most of the species found in the Red Sea: manta rays, pelagic fish, grunts (*Plectorhynchus* sp.), and the endemic *Pomacanthus asfus* with their beautiful blue-and-yellow colors. You may even have an encounter with some of the bottlenose dolphins that live here (though they are not usually very approachable) or with a large school of barracuda or batfish. While there are few sharks around during the day, night dives are not recommended because dangerous tiger sharks emerge to feed after dark.

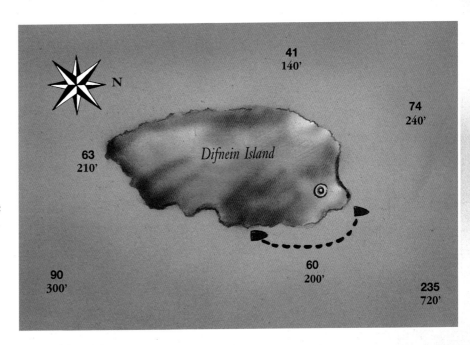

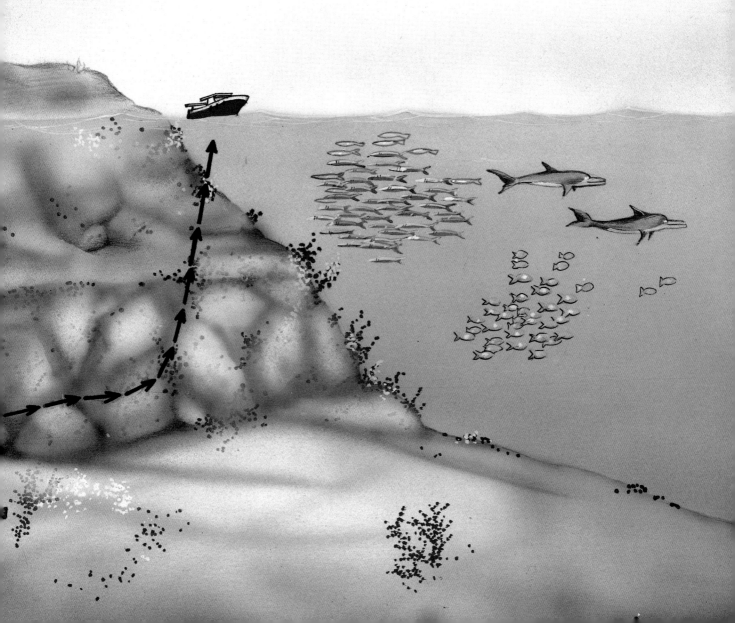

Seil Island

BY ANDREA GHISOTTI

S eil is quite close to the eastern coast of Dissei, which is only 20 miles (32 kilometers) from Massawa, so it is one of the easiest islands to reach by renting a local vessel. This small and rocky islet pulsates with birds: herons, storks, fish hawks, terns, seagulls, pelicans, wild doves, and the spoonbills that nest on the western shore.

Underwater, it is a strange little island. The water is green, not very clear, and the whole dive is quite eerie and gloomy. The best area for diving is the northern side, where the bed drops at first to a depth of 50 feet (15 meters), with huge boulders piled up to form dens. Swim to the northeast and the bottom drops to 100 feet (30 meters); swim north again to a small promontory, which plunges to 165 feet (50 meters) in a straight drop. Follow this ridge to the

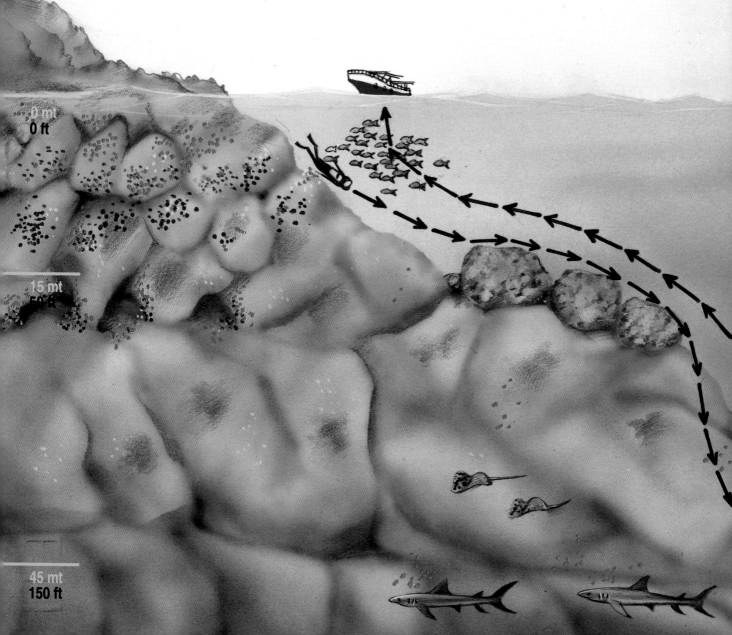

0 mt
0 ft

15 mt
50 ft

45 mt
150 ft

north and you will see a peculiar seabed, made up of vertical fissures and cracks marked off by rock blades, where fish crowd in incredible numbers. Sharks are very common in these waters, as are large red snappers, spotted rays, twobar anemone-fish, and starfish. In the coastal waters at the end of the dive you will find a teeming aquarium of small reef fish, which make great photographs.

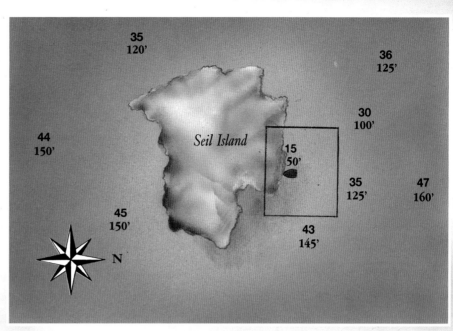

Mojeidi Island

BY ANDREA GHISOTTI

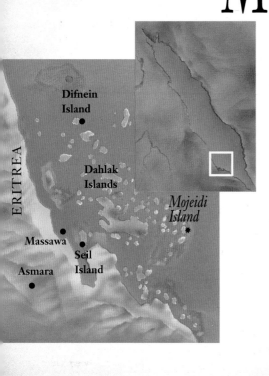

Mojeidi is the easternmost of the Dahlak Islands, extending out into the Red Sea 80 miles (130 kilometers) from Massawa—a considerable journey by ship. It is an unspoiled paradise for a great many species of animals. The beach, a marvelous span of white sand over half a mile (1 kilometer) in length, is a favorite egg-laying location for sea turtles, which land during the night in great numbers. Every morning, you can see the turtle tracks in the sand, and every night you will probably see a few of the turtles themselves. There are a number of coral constructions just off the beach, where you will see considerable varieties of smaller fish. Manta rays and eagle rays also swim in this shallow water.

The best diving is off the southeastern side. About 160 feet (50 meters) off shore, there is a small ridge about 16 feet (5 meters) in size, ending on the sandy

bottom at 40 to 50 feet (12 to 15 meters). Coral constructions are at their largest and most abundant in the area of this ridge, forming dens and caves that are well populated with crustaceans and fish of all kinds. Biologists will find the macro-fauna particularly interesting. The specialty of Mojeidi, apart from the sea turtles and eagle rays, are numerous yellow snappers that can be found in groups of up to several hundred.

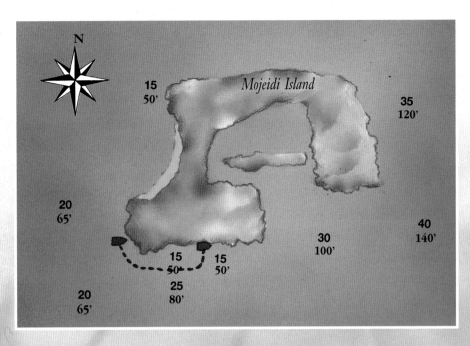

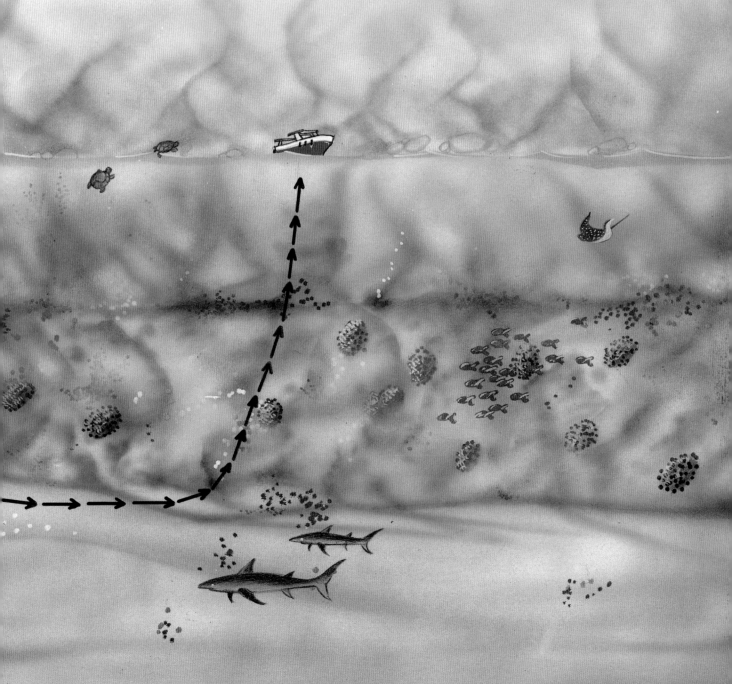

THE FISH
OF THE
RED SEA

The Red Sea is long, narrow, and extremely deep, and its coral reefs are generally set parallel to the coast, along the brinks of deep abysses. The seabeds, shallower than 165 feet (50 meters), get enough light to allow microalgae to flourish, which allows coral to prosper and form seabound "oases." These long lush bands of life take up only a fifth of the sea's surface area, so competition for space has led to a remarkable development of fauna—an incredible aquarium. In just a few square meters, you will find an exceptional variety of invertebrates (gorgonians and soft corals) and up to 20 species of fish at once. There are 1,000 species of fish in the Red Sea, and perhaps 20% of them cannot be found anywhere else on the planet. Some recent estimates actually put that number at 30%.

The coral reefs undergo an inevitable and continuous process of change and growth, though it may be just a few millimeters annually. They are jagged, riddled with fissures and crevices. They are dotted with formations shaped like columns, mushrooms, and umbrellas, which provide limitless habitats to underwater organisms.

These reefs are ideal places for predators to wait in ambush, or for prey organisms to hide from predators. Other organisms carry on extraordinary interspecies relationships here, such as that between anemones and anemone-fish; spawn can be effectively concealed and protected here. But all forms of life find food here—herbivores, scavengers, omnivores, and specialized carnivores. Many factors in the water affect the gradients of differentiation: for instance, depth, dynamics, lighting, and temperature.

Only a series of dives can provide insight into the relations that exist among the various species of fish and the many forms of adaptation, the most distinctive of which must be connected to the astounding variety of color. These colors are vivid to the human eye, but often serve as camouflage to the fish. For example, the common ocellar spots and the dark bands often covering fishes' eyes, particularly butterflyfish, serve to deceive attacking predators, who take the spots for real eyes and miss the target. Likewise, the butterflyfish's bright colors, dots, stripes, and layers of garish color make its outline incomprehensible, mingling it with the branches of coral or the lacy branches of gorgonians. The colors also transmit specific messages, such as "I am ready for reproduction," "I am dangerous," or "I am inedible." Groupers, likewise, can shift their coloring rapidly when threatened, fearful, or relaxed. In fact, marine biologists refer to the patterns that certain fish take on during an evening's rest as "pajama colorings," which can be so different from daytime colors that their species has been misidentified. In other cases, especially among the Labridae (genera *Thalassoma, Cheilinus, Gomphosus*) or the parrotfish (*Scarus* sp.), the colors can pinpoint the sex and age of individual specimens. In quite a few species, the colors distinguish adults from their young, which prevents intraspecies combat.

The colors of undersea life forms attract human attention, but do not forget that the fish of the Red Sea can be dangerous. The old saying "Look, but don't touch" is an ironclad rule for scuba divers. Not only will it help protect the environment from you, but it will also protect you from expertly camouflaged dangers in the environment.

Sharks are probably the most obvious danger to humans in the Red Sea, mainly whitetip reef sharks, blacktip reef sharks, shortnose blackfins, and silvertip sharks. They are small and considered innocuous, but it is best to be careful. Far more dangerous are the stonefish, whose camouflage renders them almost invisible, and the scorpionfish, whose long fin rays are poisonous. Scorpionfish swim slowly and are easy to approach, but they can turn and strike swiftly when they feel threatened. Surgeonfish and triggerfish are equally dangerous, though sometimes underestimated. Surgeonfish have razor-sharp spines that can cause painful cuts to unsuspecting scuba divers, and triggerfish will use their sharp teeth and powerful jaws to protect their spawn from anyone or anything they see as a threat. Even your wet suit isn't protection enough from a triggerfish's bite.

To describe the Red Sea's enormous variety of fish species individually is a colossal task not attempted here. The following pages present a selection of the most common species, those most representative of the orders and families in the Red Sea.

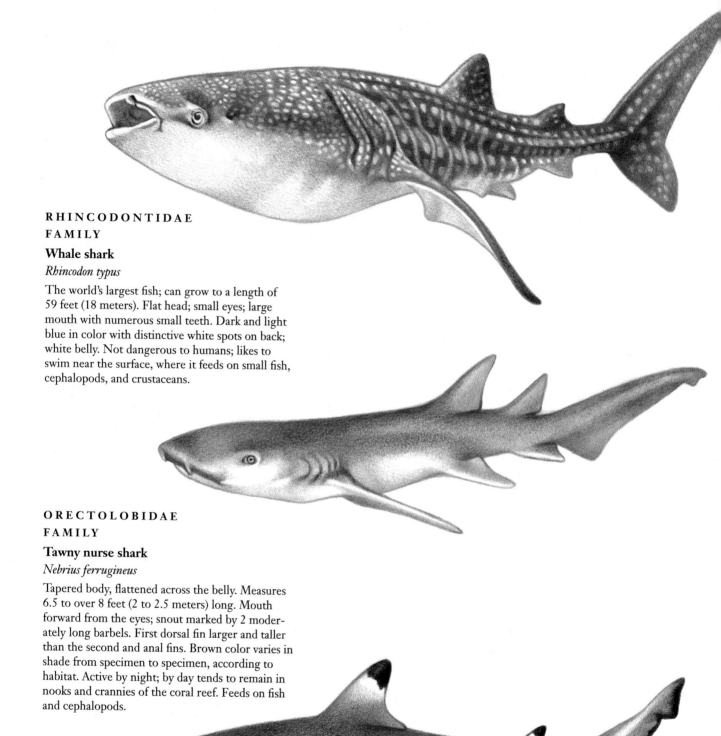

RHINCODONTIDAE FAMILY

Whale shark
Rhincodon typus

The world's largest fish; can grow to a length of 59 feet (18 meters). Flat head; small eyes; large mouth with numerous small teeth. Dark and light blue in color with distinctive white spots on back; white belly. Not dangerous to humans; likes to swim near the surface, where it feeds on small fish, cephalopods, and crustaceans.

ORECTOLOBIDAE FAMILY

Tawny nurse shark
Nebrius ferrugineus

Tapered body, flattened across the belly. Measures 6.5 to over 8 feet (2 to 2.5 meters) long. Mouth forward from the eyes; snout marked by 2 moderately long barbels. First dorsal fin larger and taller than the second and anal fins. Brown color varies in shade from specimen to specimen, according to habitat. Active by night; by day tends to remain in nooks and crannies of the coral reef. Feeds on fish and cephalopods.

CARCHARHINIDAE FAMILY

Blacktip reef shark
Carcharhinus melanopterus

Moderately sized carcharhinid at 6.5 feet (2 meters). Elongated body; flat head; short, rounded snout; triangular teeth; black fin tips. Seems to have territorial behavior; commonly seen in shallow coastal waters, especially near open-sea reefs.

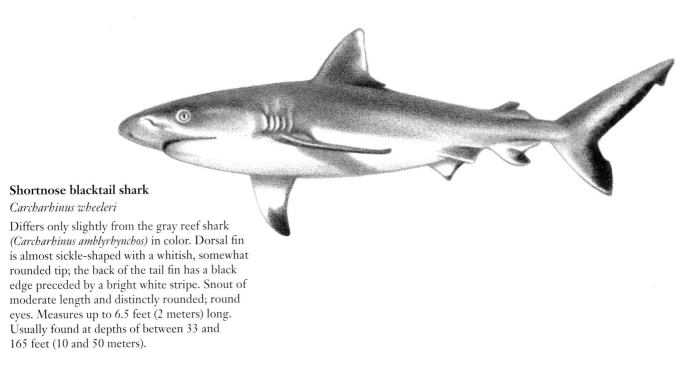

Shortnose blacktail shark
Carcharhinus wheeleri

Differs only slightly from the gray reef shark
(*Carcharhinus amblyrhynchos*) in color. Dorsal fin
is almost sickle-shaped with a whitish, somewhat
rounded tip; the back of the tail fin has a black
edge preceded by a bright white stripe. Snout of
moderate length and distinctly rounded; round
eyes. Measures up to 6.5 feet (2 meters) long.
Usually found at depths of between 33 and
165 feet (10 and 50 meters).

Whitetip reef shark
Triaenodon obesus

Tips of dorsal and tail fins are white; upper lobe of
tail fin is elongated. Small teeth; eyes have nictitat-
ing membranes. Grows up to 6.5 feet (2 meters)
long; considered by some to be harmless, tending
to shy away from humans. Do not underestimate
this shark: it seems to have territorial behavior and
many people maintain that it is actually dangerous
to humans.

SPHYRNIDAE FAMILY
Great hammerhead
Sphyrna mokarran

The head is distinguished by three slight concavities.
(The smaller, more common scalloped hammerhead [*S. lewini*] has a convex front edge.) Dorsal
fin is tall and pointed with a concave rear edge.
Found at depths of 262 feet (80 meters). Seems
to migrate, perhaps as part of the reproductive
process. Dozens of great hammerheads have been
seen swimming together.

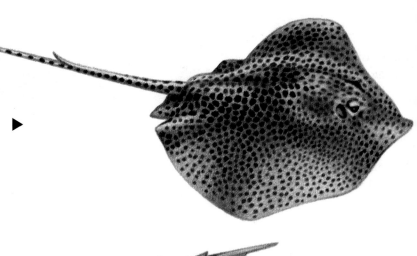

DASYATIDAE FAMILY
Coachwhip ray
Hymanthura uarnak

Disc-shaped body can be up to 6.5 feet (2 meters) in diameter, slightly wider than it is long; pointed snout. Tail 3 to 4 times longer than body, decorated with 30 to 35 dark rings; bears a poisonous spine. Back has a brownish yellow color with a number of black spots that, in some cases, merge into a network; marked by a series of tubercles that become particularly distinct between the eyes. Found in relatively shallow waters, between 3 and 16.5 feet (1 to 5 meters) deep, on sandy bottoms between reefs.

Bluespotted stingray
Taeniura lymma

Elongated, disc-shaped body, unadorned in the young but marked by a series of denticles at the center of the back in adults. Gray or yellow-brown back with blue spots; light-colored belly. Blue stripes along sides of tail; 1 or 2 poisonous spines at tip. Body about 3 feet (1 meter) wide; can grow to an overall length of more than 6.5 feet (2 meters). Lives on sandy bottoms at the base of reefs.

MYLOBATIDAE FAMILY
Spotted eagle ray
Aetobatus narinari

Easily identified by pointed, convex head with large eyes and broad lateral spiracles. Diamond-shaped body with broad, pointed pectoral fins. Measures up to 6.5 feet (2 meters) wide and can reach a total length of up to 8 feet (2.5 meters). Tail about 3 times longer than body with 1, 2, or 3 denticulated spines. Back is dark in color, with many small white spots; ventral fins broad and fleshy. Found in shallow lagoons, between 3 and 16.5 feet (1 to 5 meters) deep, on sandy bottoms.

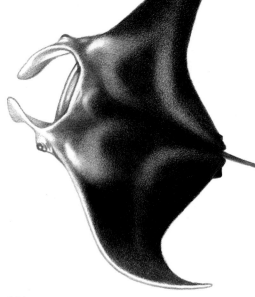

MOBULIDAE FAMILY
Giant manta
Manta birostris

Easily recognized by well-developed pectoral fins up to 19.5 feet (6 meters) in width; long, slim, spineless tail. Head projects from body and is distinguished by a pair of long, flat, flexible cephalic fins, separated by the large arch of the mouth; upper jaw devoid of teeth. Dark dorsal coloring; ventral coloring quite light with dark blotches that serve to distinguish one specimen from another.

SYNODONTIDAE FAMILY
Lizardfish
Synodus variegatus

Elongated body, compressed lengthwise. Head convex toward the rear base; eyes in an anterior-dorsal position; short, pointed snout; wide, slightly oblique mouth; well-developed jaws with numerous needle-shaped teeth. Variable coloring, generally brownish on the back with more or less distinct red spots on the sides. Prefers sandy bottoms, where it waits in ambush, poised on its sizable ventral fins.

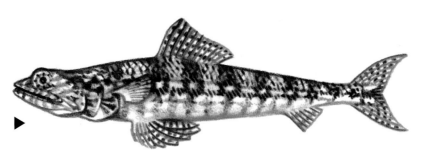

MURAENIDAE FAMILY
Gray moray
Siderea grisa

Small moray with tapered body; small snout with well-hidden nares. Measures up to 18 inches (45 centimeters). Mouth has conical teeth, more numerous on upper jaw. Brownish head with series of aligned black points on back and between the eyes; rest of body pale brown with violet nuances and brownish marbling. Young are lighter in color. Commonly seen in open meadowlands.

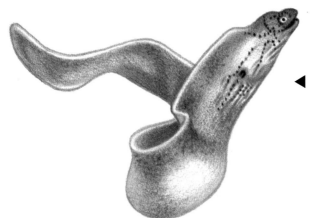

Giant moray
Gymnothorax javanicus

Largest of the morays; fairly common across the Red Sea. Powerful body; tall in the trunk; very well developed head; reticulated tail. Short snout; wide mouth; large, black, obvious openings to the opercules. Body marked by 3 rows of dark brown spots. Can grow to more than 8 feet (2.5 meters) long.

PLOTOSIDAE FAMILY
Striped eel catfish
Plotosus lineatus

Easily recognized by 4 barbels surrounding its mouth. Second dorsal, caudal, and anal fin connected. Adults have dark backs with 2 white longitudinal stripes and can measure 14 inches (35 centimeters) long. Young have bright yellow barbels and fins. Dorsal and pectoral fins have serrated spinous rays connected with poison glands. *Do not handle these fish.* Tends to be social; found along coastal reefs and near meadowlands.

FISTULARIIDAE FAMILY
Cornetfish
Fistularia commersoni

Cylindrical body; long, tubular snout. Measures up to 5 feet (1.5 meters) long. Dorsal and anal fins symmetrical and set quite far back. The 2 central rays of caudal fin are very fine and elongated. Variable coloring—remarkable capacity for camouflage used to ambush small prey. Commonly swims alongside a larger, harmless fish to further hide from prey.

ANTENNARIIDAE FAMILY

Frogfish

Antennarius coccineus

Stout, rounded body; rather tall; clumsy swimmer; moves slowly, sometimes using pectoral and ventral fins to "walk" on the seabed. Particularly distinctive transformation of the first ray on the dorsal fin, used as bait to attract prey. Variable coloring; always well camouflaged. Lives among coral reefs, sometimes clutching to branches with pectoral fins.

ANOMALOPIDAE FAMILY

Flashlight fish

Photoblepharon palpebratus

Oval-shaped body; short snout; truncated forward profile. Dark gray in color. Measures up to 4 inches (10 centimeters) long. Nocturnal habits; extremely well-developed eyes above a large, elliptical light-generating organ that contains luminescent bacteria; can extinguish light by lowering a flap of skin.

HOLOCENTRIDAE FAMILY

Blotcheye soldierfish

Myripristis murdjan

Oval body; moderately compressed and high; covered with bright red stinging scales. Measures up to 12 inches (30 centimeters) long. First dorsal fin has 10 well-developed spinous rays. Large eyes; wide mouth. Nocturnal habits; keeps watch at grotto entrance during the day.

Crown squirrelfish

Adioryx diadema

Oval body, longer than flashlight fish at 10 inches (25 centimeters), but not as tall. Nocturnal habits; large eyes. Red with white stripes on the sides; white band around lower portion of the face to the opercules; forward section of dorsal fin is black.

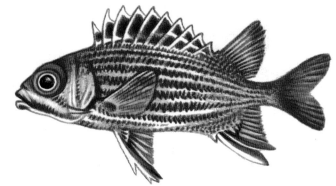

Saber squirrelfish

Adioryx spinifer

Tall, moderately compressed body; pointed snout; relatively large eyes. Measures up to 18 inches (45 centimeters) long. Well-developed dorsal fin with red interradial membranes. Red body with red spots; darker on the opercula and at base of pectoral fins. Nocturnal habits; aggressive and territorial.

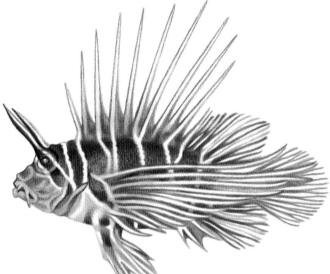

Tailbar lionfish

Pterois radiata

Oblong body; large head; large mouth. Very long pectoral fin rays that do not branch out; upper rays joined by a membrane at the base; all rays are poisonous. Brownish red body with white stripes. Long, fleshy papillae above the eyes. Measures up to 10 inches (25 centimeters) long.

Lionfish

Pterois volitans

Body similar to squirrelfish. Broad brown vertical stripes of various widths. Fin rays have a more or less developed membrane similar to feathers; every other fin has rows of brownish black spots. Indented appendages around the mouth and above the eyes.

Devil scorpionfish

Scorpaenopsis diabolus

Slightly oval body, massive and high, with numerous fleshy excrescences. Measures up to 12 inches (30 centimeters) long. Large head covered with spines; wide, upturned mouth. Pectoral fins extend to anal fin. Excellent camouflage; hunts by ambush. Tail fin has broad, dark vertical stripes. Spines of dorsal fin are poisonous, but not to the same degree as those of the stonefish.

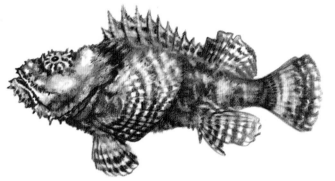

Stonefish

Synanceia verrucosa

Moderately oblong body; compressed at sides; free of scales. Massive head covered with crests and spines. Very obvious eyes turn upward, as does the mouth. Very well-developed pectoral fins. Excellent camouflage; virtually indistinguishable from a stone. Glands at base of spines produce a very powerful, sometimes fatal poison.

Crocodile fish

Cociella crocodilus

Body compressed at the front and slightly cylindrical to the rear; covered with rough scales. Measures up to 27 inches (70 centimeters) long. Large mouth, well lined with small, sharp teeth. There are 2 dorsal fins; first one is preceded by an isolated spine; caudal fin is rounded. Coloring ranges from brownish to olive gray, with dark spots on the back. Usually found on seabed or partly buried in silt, alone or in pairs.

Scalefin anthias

Anthias squamipinnis

Oval, compressed body; sickle-shaped tail with elongated lobes. Measures up to 6.5 inches (17 centimeters) long. Short, rounded snout; terminal mouth. Well-developed dorsal fin, especially in the male, which has several particularly long fore rays. Reddish color with red spots near the pectoral fins. Females have yellowish shadings. Gregarious, forming schools dominated by one or two males.

Peacock grouper

Cephalopholis argus

Massive, tapered body, slightly compressed. Measures up to 20 inches (50 centimeters) long. Powerful head; slightly prominent lower jaw. Rounded edge on caudal fin; dorsal fin has 9 spinous rays and rounded rear edge that ends near the caudal peduncle opposite the anal fin. Marked by numerous dark blue spots and 10 dark bands on the sides; dark blue fins.

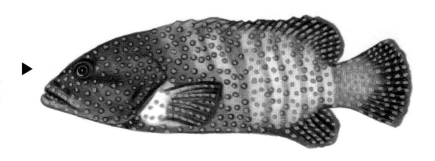

Coral grouper

Cephalopholis miniata

Body similar to that of peacock grouper; rear edges of dorsal and anal fins less rounded. Measures up to 18 inches (45 centimeters) long. Very bright reddish orange color; many small, dark blue ocellate spots scattered all over the body and fins; adults tend to be darker. Fairly territorial; prefers to remain in the general vicinity of grottoes. Tends to become more gregarious during mating season, gathering in restricted areas.

Lunartail grouper

Variola louti

Tapered body, terminating in a tall caudal peduncle. Peduncle supports an unmistakable tail, which is in the form of a crescent moon with elongated lobes. Fairly common species; measures up to 33 inches (85 centimeters). Dorsal and anal fins have pointed rear edges. Reddish or brownish color, with purple highlights and numerous pale spots.

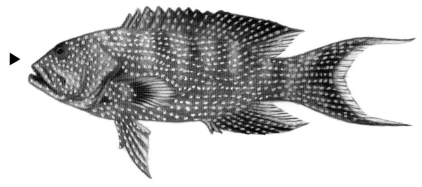

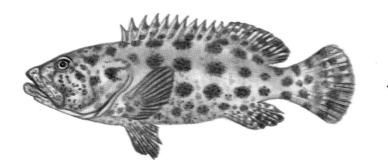

Potato cod
Epinephelus tukula

Broad, powerful body; tapered head with a convex intraorbital space; elongated snout; wide mouth; lower jaw more developed than upper. Can grow to more than 6.5 feet (2 meters) long. Gray-brown in color, with large, pronounced dark spots along the sides and on the tail. Fins marked by smaller, more numerous spots.

Giant grouper
Epinephelus tauvina

Tapered body, slightly compressed; not as tall as other groupers. Can grow to more than 6.5 feet (2 meters) long. Pointed snout; broad and terminal mouth. Rounded caudal fin; shortish dorsal fin with 11 spinous rays. A number of large dark spots at the base of the dorsal fin; smaller spots scattered along the body, which is mainly pale.

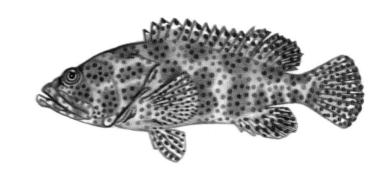

GRAMMISTIDAE FAMILY

Goldstriped goldfish
Grammistes sexlineatus

Tall, oval, compressed body, covered with many small scales. Measures up to 12 inches (30 centimeters) long. Wide mouth; lower jaw has a small fleshy excrescence. Easily recognized by a distinctive pattern of whitish yellow stripes running lengthwise from head to caudal peduncle; very noticeable against the brown-and-blue body. Secretes a mucus toxic to other fish when alarmed.

PRIACANTHIDAE FAMILY

Crescent-tail bigeye
Priacanthus hamrur

Tall, oval, compressed body; short snout; upturned mouth. Measures up to 18 inches (45 centimeters) long. Nocturnal habits; large, protruding eyes. Caudal fin shaped like a crescent moon with elongated lobes, especially in adults. Generally a dark reddish color, but capable of changing rapidly, acquiring silvery highlights or becoming striped with red on silvery body. Dorsal and anal fins have dark highlights along their edges.

CIRRHITIDAE FAMILY

Longnose hawkfish
Oxycirrhites typus

Slightly cylindrical body, taller at the center. Measures up to 5 inches (13 centimeters) long. Elongated snout; small mouth. Spinous part of dorsal fins bears a series of appendages. Pectoral fins particularly well developed: used to balance on gorgonians. A series of red stripes forming a checkerboard pattern perfectly camouflages this fish on gorgonians.

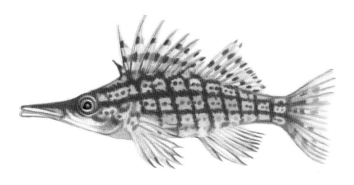

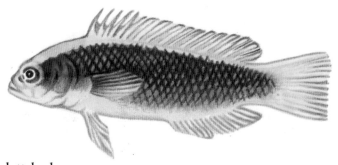

Olive dottyback
Pseudochromis fridmani

Found only in the Red Sea. Elongated body, tapered to the front. Measures up to 3 inches (7 centimeters) long. Short snout; large eyes; terminal mouth. Caudal fin truncated in the young and with a slightly more elongated lower lobe in adults. Bright purple color, almost luminescent; thin, dark band from tip of snout to eye; fairly pronounced dark blue spot on opercula; upper lobe of caudal fin practically transparent. Often found under coral umbrellas that jut from reef walls.

▶

PSEUDOCHROMIDAE FAMILY
Sunrise dottyback
Pseudochromis flavivertex

◀ Elongated, compressed body. Measures up to 4 inches (10 centimeters) long. Distinguished by a very long dorsal fin and long anal fin. Slightly protruding eyes in subdorsal position. Distinctive two-tone coloring: bright chrome yellow above, light blue elsewhere. Prefers to live among the coral branches, near a sandy bottom.

APOGONIDAE FAMILY
Golden cardinalfish
Apogon aureus

◀ Tapered body; broad mouth, head, and eyes. Measures up to 5 inches (12 centimeters) long. Two separate dorsal fins of similar size; large, pronounced scales. Head darker than body, which is pale yellow; broad, dark band surrounding caudal peduncle; dark ventral band in large specimens. Tends to be nocturnal; gathers in groups in dark locations during the day.

CARANGIDAE FAMILY
Bluefin trevally
Caranx melampygus

Rather tall, elongated body; convex head with high forehead; small eyes. Measures over 3 feet (1 meter) long. Narrow caudal peduncle reinforced with visible bony plates; lateral line complete and arched anteriorly. Greenish brown in color, with numerous small black spots. Long, sickle-shaped pectoral fins with scales on the sides, yellow in the young.

▶

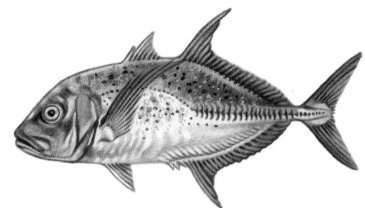

Bigeye trevally
Caranx sexfasciatus

Elongated, compressed body; rounded forward silhouette; jutting lower jaw. Can measure over 5 feet (1.5 meters) long. Evident keels on caudal stalk; sharply forked caudal fin. Blue-gray or blue-green back coloring; lobes of caudal fin show blackish hue; sides are greenish yellow or silvery. The young are golden yellow, with 4 to 7 broad dark vertical bands. ◀

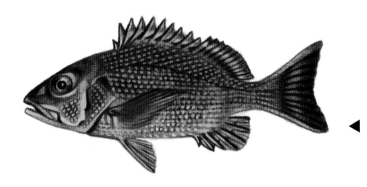

LUTJANIDAE FAMILY

Twinspot snapper

Lutjanus bohar

Elongated, tall, powerful body. Measures up to 30 inches (75 centimeters) long. Pointed snout; wide mouth lined with one row of conical teeth above and below and pronounced front canines. Well-developed fins: only one dorsal fin; sickle-shaped pectoral fins stretch almost to the anal fin. Reddish purple, darker on the back, with yellowish highlights on either side of the head; dark fins, partly edged with white; spinous rays on the dorsal fin are white at the tips.

Bluestripe snapper

Lutjanus kasmira

Tapered body; pointed snout; large eyes; large mouth. Measures 16 inches (40 centimeters) long. Dorsal fin extends to height of caudal peduncle. Golden yellow on the back, becoming gradually paler along the sides and almost silvery on the belly. Four light stripes typically run lengthwise, the longest running from mouth to caudal peduncle. Black edges on the dorsal and caudal fins.

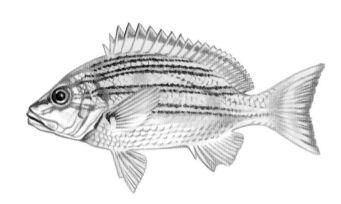

CAESIONIDAE FAMILY

Suez fusilier

Caesio suevicus

Rounded, rather elongated, tapered body; small mouth with thin teeth in front of a row of very small teeth; upper jaw can be extended forward to capture small prey. Particularly distinctive forked caudal fin. Generally silvery in color, with yellow nuances; black tail fin lobes. Tend to travel in schools. Measure up to 8 inches (20 centimeters) long.

HAEMULIDAE FAMILY

Blackspotted grunt

Plectorhynchus gaterinus

Tapered, tall, slightly compressed body; well-developed head; short, convex snout; large eyes; smallish mouth distinguished by a pair of thick lips. Adults have a basic color of bright yellow with numerous black spots. Young have 5 black longitudinal bands; the 2 bands closest to the back extend to the caudal fin. Tend to form schools close to the reef's slope during the day. Measure up to 20 inches (50 centimeters) long.

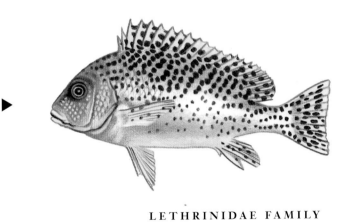

LETHRINIDAE FAMILY

Spangled emperor

Lethrinus nebulosus

Fairly tall, compressed body; elongated head with sharply oblique forward profile; pointed snout; eyes tend upward; mouth entirely red. Well-developed dorsal fin; pectoral fins have scales on the inner section. Basic color is uniform gray, enlivened by light blue stripes and spots, more evident on the sides, the opercules, and behind the eyes. Present in large numbers on open and shallow seabeds. Can grow longer than 30 inches (75 centimeters).

KYPHOSIDAE
Snubnose chub
Kyphosus cinerascens

Oval body covered with small, rough scales that extend over the head and fins. Small mouth with numerous teeth, also present on the tongue. Rounded dorsal fin, tall toward the rear; rather short pectoral fins. Bluish silver, with darker dorsal fins; silvery strip running under the eyes; a number of yellow or black stripes run along the rows of scales. Swim in schools in middle layers of water during the day. Measure up to 20 inches (50 centimeters) long.

EPHIPPIDAE FAMILY
Batfish
Platax orbicularis

Unmistakable shape: tall, compressed, discoid body, with symmetrical and well-developed anal and dorsal fins. Fins are narrower in the young and become more rounded in adults. Small mouth and eyes. Broad dark vertical bands along the sides, which disappear with age. Live in schools. Measure 20 inches (50 centimeters) long.

▶

PEMPHERIDAE FAMILY
Vanikoro sweeper
Pempheris vanicolensis

Oblong, compressed body; taller to the front and tapered to the rear. The dorsal silhouette is nearly a straight line; ventral profile is concave around the long anal fin. Tail slightly incised; wide, oblique, terminal mouth; large eyes. Nocturnal species found in large schools in the shelter of coral reefs. Light in color, pink and translucent. Measures up to 6 inches (15 centimeters) long.

MULLIDAE FAMILY
Yellowsaddle goatfish
Parupeneus cyclostomus

High, tapered body; jutting snout; lower jaw has 2 long barbels that extend to the ventral fins. The 2 dorsal fins are sharply separated. Typically 2-lobed tail. Coloring brighter in the young: head has evident bluish stripes; dark spot to the rear of the second dorsal fin. Measures up to 14 inches (35 centimeters) long.

▶

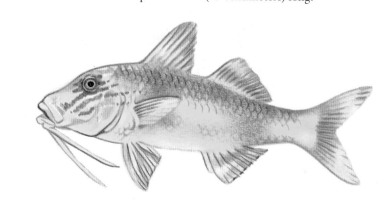

Forsskal's goatfish
Parupeneus forskali

Body shape typical of genus; barbels less pronounced than in the yellowsaddle. Silvery blue with yellow nuances on the back. Bright yellow caudal peduncle with a pronounced dark spot in the center. A dark band that covers the eye runs along the sides.

ECHENEIDAE FAMILY

Sharksucker

Echeneis naucrates

Elongated body; head flattened dorsally to accommodate a suction cup (nothing more than a modified dorsal fin). Mouth has well-developed lower jaw. Dorsal and anal fins similar and symmetrical. Dark gray or brownish with a darker band running lengthwise; whitish fin edges. Measures over 3 feet (1 meter) long.

◀

SPHYRAENIDAE FAMILY

Great barracuda

Sphyraena barracuda

Elongated, slightly cylindrical body; long, pointed snout; prominent lower jaw; numerous canine-shaped teeth. The 2 dorsal fins are sharply separated. Color ranges from grayish to greenish brown on the back, with silvery sides and belly. Adults have irregular dark spot along their sides near the caudal fin. Grows to nearly 6 feet (just under 2 meters) in length.

▶

Blackfin barracuda

Sphyraena qenie

Elongated body typical of barracuda. Prominent lower jaw devoid of any fleshy excrescence, but the back of the jaw never extends beyond the forward margin of the eye. The first dorsal fin starts after the pectoral fins; the second dorsal fin is symmetrical with the anal fin. Forked caudal fin has 3 lobes in large specimens. Silvery color, with 18 to 22 dark vertical bands; dark dorsal, caudal, and anal fins; last 2 anal rays are white. Grows to over 3 feet (1 meter) long.

▶

POMACENTRIDAE FAMILY

Sergeant major

Abdudefduf saxatilis

Compressed, ovoid, fairly tall body covered with rough scales that extend to the fins. Pointed head; short snout. Small mouth, slightly protractile, lined with conical teeth. Dorsal fin has mostly spinous rays; caudal fin is forked. Grayish silvery coloring shifts to bright yellow on the back; 5 dark vertical bands along the sides, the first of which intersects the rearmost edge of the operculum; becomes lighter on sandy seabed, and darker on coral. Adult males get blue and purple nuances when guarding their spawn. Can measure up to 6 inches (15 centimeters) long.

◀

Sergeant scissortail

Abdudefduf sexfasciatus

Configuration of the body similar to others in the species. Silvery white coloring, with 6 black bands, the first of which covers the rearmost edge of the operculum; caudal fin lobes marked by a black stripe. Gregarious; tend to live in schools near the shallow coral formations. Can grow to a length of almost 8 inches (20 centimeters).

▶

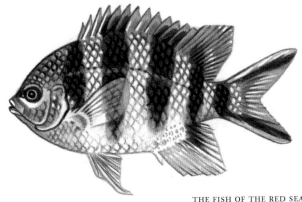

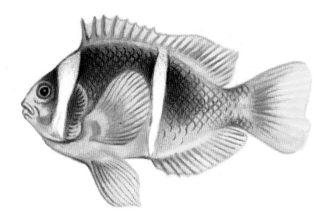

Twobar anemonefish
Amphiprion bicinctus

Oval, rounded body; short, snubbed snout; small mouth. Dorsal fin extends along much of the dorsum and presents a slight saddle formation that separates the spinous portion from the portion with the soft rays; two lobes on the caudal fin. Background coloring ranges from orange to brownish orange, with 2 white vertical stripes. Young specimens may have a third stripe on the stalk of the tail fin. Generally lives in symbiosis with anemonefish of the genus *Heteractis*. Can grow 6 inches (15 centimeters) long.

Bluegreen chromis
Chromis caerulea

Body shape roughly similar to the damselfish of the Mediterranean. Coloring is relatively intense, tends to blue, with slight nuances along the edge of the scales. Gregarious; tends to form large groups, each of which seems to colonize a specific coral formation; favors sheer walls at the outer reef edge. Measures up to 4 inches (10 centimeters) long.

Half-and-half chromis
Chromis dimidiata

Similar in shape to the bluegreen chromis; much different in color. Easily recognized by the half-brown, half-white body. Gregarious; tends to form huge schools near large coral formations, venturing to greater depths than the bluegreen chromis. Measures almost 3 inches (7 centimeters).

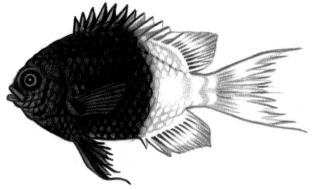

Banded dascyllus
Dascyllus aruanus

Fairly stubby, squarish, tall, compressed body. Small mouth; slightly prominent lower jaw. Whitish background coloring; 3 distinctive diagonal dark bands, the first of which covers the eye and the mouth. Forms small groups, each of which is closely associated with a single coral colony. Only larger specimens venture any distance from the corals; smaller ones remain in permanent residence among the branches. Measures up to 4 inches (10 centimeters) long.

Sulphur damselfish
Pomacentrus sulfureus

Slightly oval, tall, compressed body; short snout; small, protractile mouth lined with a number of rows of small teeth. Near the eye is a flat spine pointing backward; opercula has serrated edge; caudal fin is slightly inset. Yellow with a black spot at the base of the pectoral fins. A number of individuals can be found close together, but they do not move in large, closely packed schools. Measures up to 4 inches (10 centimeters) long.

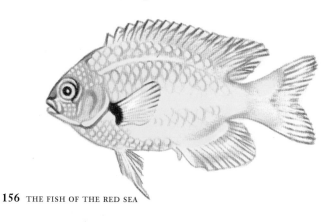

Domino damselfish
Dascyllus trimaculatus

Body shape typical of the genus. Small mouth, considering it feeds on plankton. Unmistakable coloring: either black or brown with 3 white spots, one on either side and one on the forehead. White spots more pronounced in the young, fading in adults. Common around anemonefish, long-spined black urchins, and acroporas. Measures up to 5.5 inches (14 centimeters) long.

LABRIDAE FAMILY

Yellowtail wrasse
Anampses meleagrides

Tapered body; generally oval silhouette; slight frontal hump, more pronounced in females. Terminal, protractile mouth with large, fleshy lips. Adult males are dark and purplish with more or less elongated bluish spots along the edge of the scales. Dorsal, anal, and caudal fins feature bluish stripes; elongated lobes on the caudal fin. Females are dark, spangled with numerous white spots; reddish snout and lower head; yellow caudal fin. Measures up to 10 inches (25 centimeters) long.

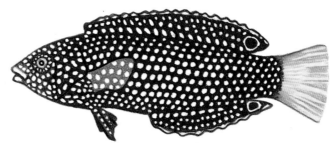

Abudjubbe wrasse
Cheilinus abudjubbe

Tall, powerful body covered with large scales. Elongated, convex head; well-developed mouth with pronounced canine-shaped teeth. Dark background coloring; darker with red spots along the sides; distinctive red stripes radiate from the eyes. Fins are lighter in color, with yellow-green spots distributed in rows along the rays. Often feeds on sea urchins. Measures 14 inches (35 centimeters) long.

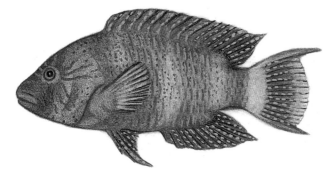

Broomtail wrasse
Cheilinus lunulatus

Tall, compressed body with large scales and convex, stubby head. Large, protractile mouth. Males have a relatively dark background coloring, especially on the head, with purple stripes that are sometimes particularly pronounced along the edges of the scales. Yellow pectoral fins; bluish nuances around the mouth and fins; short caudal fin has fringed rear edge peculiar to the species. Measures up to 18 inches (50 centimeters) long.

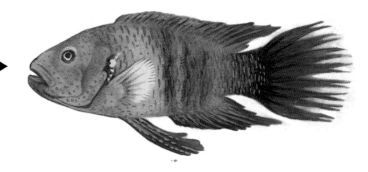

Humphead wrasse
Cheilinus undulatus

The largest known member of the family with a very distinctive tall and stubby structure. Large mouth with thick protractile lips that allow prey literally to be sucked up. In adults, the head is marked by a pronounced bump on the forehead. Greenish gray with irregular greenish yellow stripes along the sides, shifting to orange on the head. Can grow as long as 6.5 feet (2 meters) and weigh more than 400 pounds (180 kilograms).

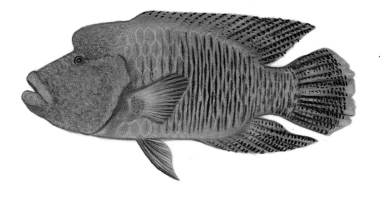

Eightline wrasse
Paracheilinus octotaenia

Tapered body; rounded forward profile. Remarkable development of dorsal and anal fins differentiate it from typical Labridae: they are rounded, quite high, and almost joined to the fan-shaped caudal fin in the rear. Yellowish body marked by 8 bluish horizontal lines; bright red fins with white edges. Measures up to 5 inches (12 centimeters) long.

African coris
Coris gaimard

Tapered, slender body, with a silhouette reminiscent of the Mediterranean rainbow wrasse. The first two rays on the dorsal fin are general elongated in adults. Reddish coloring features fine greenish stripes at the base of each scale; greenish head with broad greenish bands, the widest of which runs from the rear edge of the mouth to the operculum. Males have a green stripe along the side, just above the point of origin of the anal fin. Reaches a length of up to 16 inches (40 centimeters).

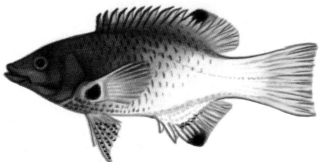

Axilspot hogfish
Bodianus axillaris

Tapered, compressed body; pointed snout. Well-developed ventral fins; the longer ventral rays reach almost to the anal aperture. Caudal fin truncated in adults and rounded in the young. Forward portion of the body is dark and contrasts sharply with the lighter color of the rest of the body. The base of the pectoral, dorsal, and anal fins has a pronounced dark spot. Young specimens have 9 white spots on their bodies. Measures up to 8 inches (20 centimeters) long.

Red Sea bird wrasse
Gomphosus caeruleus

Typically oval, slightly compressed body. Distinctively elongated snout, tubular in adults. Terminal mouth, sufficiently well developed to prey on small animals. Rounded caudal fin tends to develop elongated lobes with time. Males are dark blue; females have green backs and yellow bellies, with black spots on the sides. Measure up to 10 inches (25 centimeters) long.

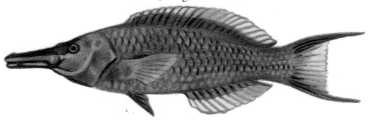

Cleaner wrasse
Labroides dimidiatus

Elongated, compressed body with large scales. Pointed head; elongated snout; terminal mouth lined with numerous small and pointed teeth; upper jaw longer than lower. Front half of the body is brownish, darker on the back than on the belly; a broad black band runs from the beginning of the snout to the tip of the caudal fin, widening as it goes. The base of the anal fin and the rear part of the body are an intense dark blue. Measures up to 4 inches (10 centimeters) long.

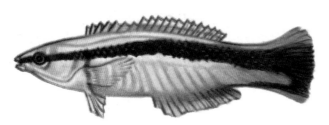

Klunzinger's wrasse
Thalassoma klunzingeri

Tapered, powerful, slightly compressed, elongated body. Small mouth with 2 clearly visible canine-shaped front teeth; thin lips. Greenish body with fairly dark reddish brown stripes along the scales and on the lobes of the caudal fin. Head marked by broad and pronounced reddish brown stripes, especially between the eyes and gullet. Grows up to 8 inches (20 centimeters) in length.

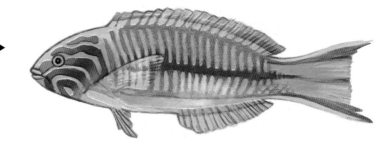

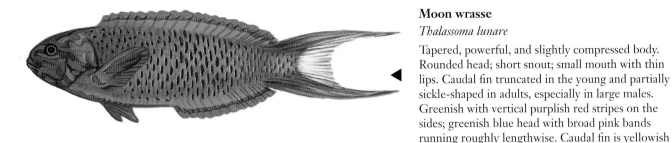

Moon wrasse
Thalassoma lunare

Tapered, powerful, and slightly compressed body. Rounded head; short snout; small mouth with thin lips. Caudal fin truncated in the young and partially sickle-shaped in adults, especially in large males. Greenish with vertical purplish red stripes on the sides; greenish blue head with broad pink bands running roughly lengthwise. Caudal fin is yellowish at the center with pink stripes along the lobes. Measures up to 12 inches (30 centimeters) long.

SCARIDAE FAMILY

Rusty parrotfish
Scarus ferrugineus

Tapered body, slightly compressed at the sides, covered with large scales. Large head; terminal mouth; slightly prominent upper jaw; distinctively large teeth that join to form a beak of 4 plates. The male, with a greenish snout and fins edged in blue-green, is more colorful than the female. Prefers a protected coral seabed. Grows up to 16 inches (40 centimeters) long.

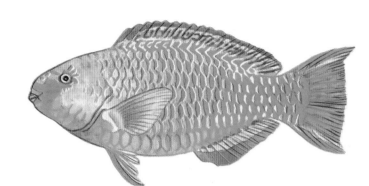

Steephead parrotfish
Scarus gibbus

Oval, tall, powerful body. Head has a convex, nearly vertical forward silhouette; dental plates not particularly pronounced; 3 rows of large scales on the cheeks. Semilunar caudal fin; green at the rear edge. Brownish yellow coloring with fairly intense pink stripes on the scales; blue-green ventral section. The lower snout is green in females; males have a greenish coloring with touches of violet on their dorsal area. Grows up to 28 inches (70 centimeters) long.

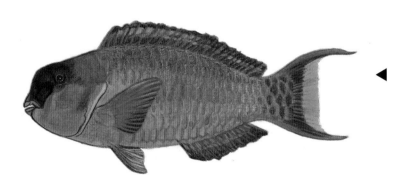

Bullethead parrotfish
Scarus sordidus

Body configuration typical of parrotfish; dental plates can be seen clearly. The young present a pattern of horizontal stripes. As they grow, the coloring turns dark brown. Adult males are green with salmon pink edges to their scales; cheeks are bright orange, fading to yellow on the opercula. Strangely, their teeth are green, which goes nicely with the pink mouth found on females.

Bumphead parrotfish
Bolbometopon muricatum

Powerful, tall body; compressed at the sides and covered with large scales. Three rows of scales occur at the sides of the snout and near the mouth. Males and females are greenish blue with pink snouts and gullets. Males can be recognized by the pink forward portion of the prominence. The young are dark brown, with a double row of white spots along the upper half of the body. Can grow up to 5 feet (1.5 meters) long.

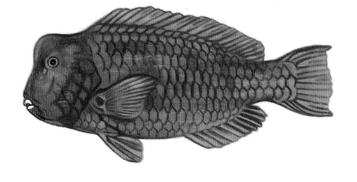

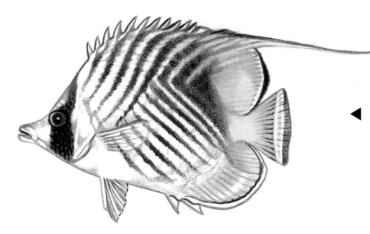

Threadfin butterflyfish
Chaetodon auriga

Nearly rectangular, very tall, compressed body; head concave toward the front; short, pointed snout. A broad dark band covers the eye, narrowing on the back. Dark ocellate spot along the back edge of the dorsal fin, topped by a number of elongated and filamentous rays—the most distinctive feature of this species. Swims alone or in pairs. Measures up to 10 inches (25 centimeters) long.

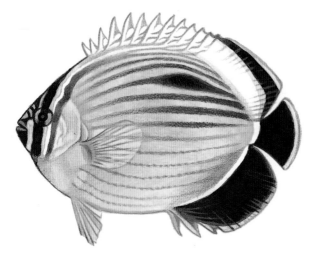

Exquisite butterflyfish
Chaetodon austriacus

Typically oval, compressed body; short snout; very long dorsal fin; well-developed anal fin. The rear edges of the dorsal and anal fins seem to shade into the caudal fin. Background color is yellow with a series of slightly diagonal blue-black stripes along the sides. The snout is dark, and a vertical black stripe completely covers the eye. The anal fin, caudal fin, and rear edge of the dorsal fin are black. Feeds entirely on polyps. Measures up to 5 inches (12 centimeters) long.

Striped butterflyfish
Chaetodon fasciatus

Body shape similar to the exquisite butterflyfish. Background coloring is yellow; 9 or 10 slightly diagonal bands of dark color run along the sides, merging into a single band of the same color parallel to the dorsal fin. The dorsal, caudal, and anal fins are trimmed with a brownish yellow band; the black eye band is followed by a shorter white band. Measures up to 7 inches (18 centimeters) long.

Blackback butterflyfish
Chaetodon melannotus

Nearly oval, tall, compressed body; head has oblique and slightly concave forward profile; short, pointed snout. Most distinctive feature is the black band that cuts vertically across the snout, covering the eye. All the fins are yellow; the rear portion of the caudal peduncle and forward portion of the anal fin have black spots. Diagonal rows of points that converge into a dark dorsal band on the sides. Measures up to 7 inches (18 centimeters) long.

Paleface butterflyfish
Chaetodon mesoleucos

Tall, slightly square body, extremely compressed laterally; convex forward profile; short snout. White forward portion; brown rear portion; 12 black vertical stripes. Black caudal fin trimmed in white, with a whitish, orange-tipped crescent. Upper silhouette of the snout marked by a black band that covers the eye. Measures up to 6 inches (16 centimeters) long.

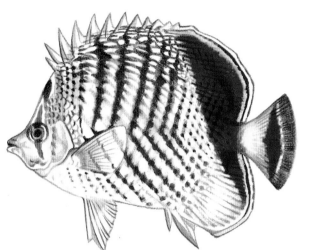

Crown butterflyfish
Chaetodon paucifasciatus

Tall, compressed body; pointed snout. Background color is quite pale; forward section is whitish with a strip of tawny reddish yellow covering the eye. Four or 5 bands of black diamond shapes mark the sides; distinctive red spot on the rear part of the body; a band of red distinguishes the caudal fin. There is an ocellar dot at the center of the red spot in the young. Generally swims in pairs or in small groups near the meadowlands. Measures up to 5.5 inches (14 centimeters) long.

Masked butterflyfish
Chaetodon semilarvatus

This species is peculiar to the Red Sea. Almost discoid in shape; small, prominent snout. Almost uniformly orange-yellow with fine dark diagonal stripes. A dark bluish spot surrounds the eye and extends to the operculum; a dark narrow line underscores the outline of the dorsal and anal fins; the pectoral fins are transparent; the ventral fins are yellow. Often found in schools. Measures up to 8 inches (20 centimeters) long.

Pennantfish
Heniochus intermedius

Tall, disc-shaped, extremely compressed body; small head; slightly elongated snout. A broad black band marks the forward portion of the body, covers the eye and operculum, and extends to the base of the dorsal fin. A second band runs diagonally along the rear portion of the body, starting from the caudal peduncle. The spinous ray of the dorsal fin is like a banner. Measures up to 10 inches (25 centimeters) long.

Red Sea bannerfish
Heniochus diphreutes

Tall, disc-shaped, extremely compressed body, truncated in the rear. Head has concave profile; snout short; large eyes. Whitish with 2 broad dark bands on the sides, which limit the higher and more developed part of the dorsal fin, well extended behind. A dark band partially covers the eyes; yellow rear sections of dorsal and caudal fins. Swims in large schools of several dozen, its main distinction from the pennantfish. Feeds on plankton, unlike most butterflyfish. Measures up to 6 inches (16 centimeters) long.

Orangeface butterflyfish
Gonochaetodon larvatus

Tall, oval, compressed body, reminiscent of angelfish. Snout is orange from the root of the dorsal fin to the base of the ventral fins. Main body color is glistening light blue, with a number of angular white stripes. Another white line spans the tip of the dorsal fin to the caudal peduncle; black caudal peduncle and caudal fin. Commonly found near the tops of madrepores. Measures up to 4 inches (10 centimeters) long.

POMACANTHIDAE FAMILY
Arabian angelfish
Pomacanthus asfur

Tall, compressed body; head has convex forward profile; short snout; slightly prominent lower jaw. Well-developed dorsal and anal fins with rays extending long past the rear margin of the caudal fin. The coloring of the young, with vertical whitish yellow stripes, becomes a uniform dark blue in adults. Adults are distinguished by the large yellow spot on the sides that extends to part of the back and tail.

Emperor angelfish
Pomacanthus imperator

Nearly oval body; head has practically rectilinear forward profile; very short snout. Dorsal and anal fins have a rounded forward edge that just exceeds the caudal stalk. Adults feature many diagonal yellow bands; eyes are masked by a black stripe edged in light blue, followed by a similar stripe on the operculum. Measures up to 14 inches (35 centimeters) long.

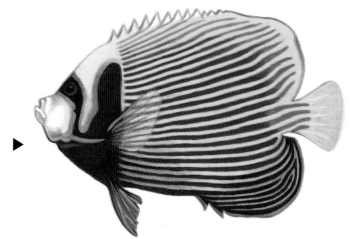

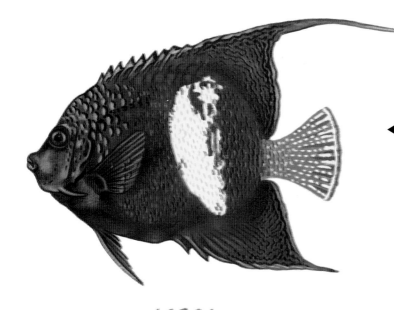

Yellowbar angelfish
Pomacanthus maculosus

Body shape similar to the Arabian angelfish. The young have light vertical stripes on the sides and a pale, translucent caudal fin. Adults have a large yellow spot on the side, which does not extend to the dorsal area. Tends to be solitary. Measures up to 12 inches (30 centimeters) long.

Royal angelfish
Pygoplites diacanthus

Body not as tall as that of the typical angelfish. The rear edges of the dorsal and anal fins are well developed, but do not exceed the caudal fin. Background coloring of orange-yellow with 8 or 9 dark blue bands; eyes are surrounded by 2 sharply defined dark blue stripes. Dorsal fin has a fairly dark vermiculation; anal fin has parallel yellow stripes along the edge. The young are fairly similar, with a posterior ocellar spot. Measures up to 12 inches (30 centimeters) long.

ACANTHURIDAE FAMILY

Black surgeonfish
Acanthurus nigricans

Oval, tall, slightly compressed body; rounded forward profile. Well-developed dorsal and anal fins; sickle-shaped caudal fin with elongated lobes, distinguished by a white band at its base; short black band behind the eyes alongside the spines of the caudal peduncle; pectoral fins have a dark yellow border. Measures up to 16 inches (40 centimeters) long.

Brown surgeonfish
Acanthurus nigrofuscus

Oval, tall, compressed body; extremely convex forward profile; short snout; black lips; concave caudal fin. Dark brown or purplish brown, with or without thin bluish gray lines running lengthwise along the side. Rear edges of the anal and dorsal fins distinguished by a black spot; numerous orange spots on head and chin; spine on the peduncle is bordered in black. Measures up to 8 inches (20 centimeters) long.

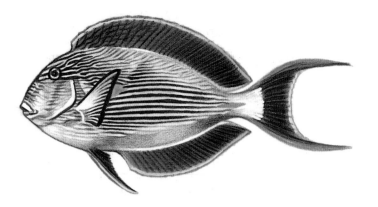

Sohal surgeonfish
Acanthurus sohal

Oval, tall, compressed body; rounded, powerful head; mouth has thick lips and spatulate teeth suited to grazing on algae. Blue-gray, with numerous dark stripes along the side and upper part of the head; white cheeks; dark fins edged with a light blue band. The fearsome spines on the caudal peduncle are distinguished by their bright orange color. Very territorial behavior. Measures up to 16 inches (40 centimeters) long.

Spotted unicornfish
Naso brevirostris

The most distinctive of the surgeonfish: a powerful oval body terminating in a long beak that extends well beyond the snout. There are 2 bony plates, each with a sharp spine, on the sides of the peduncle. Rounded caudal fin. Grayish blue to olive brown coloring; lips sometimes blue; tail has a pale band along the lower edge. Gregarious habits. Measures up to 20 inches (50 centimeters) long.

Orangespine unicornfish
Naso literatus

Oval, compressed body, tall at the front; powerful head; dorsal profile forms a 45° angle; pointed snout; small mouth lined with sharp teeth. There are 2 bony plates, each with a sharp, forward-curving spine, on the sides of the peduncle. The caudal fin is semilunar, with pointed lobes and long filamentous rays. Yellowish brown general coloring; orange caudal peduncle; light yellow spot between the eyes; yellowish orange dorsal fin, black at the base, with a white edge. Measures up to 18 inches (45 centimeters) long.

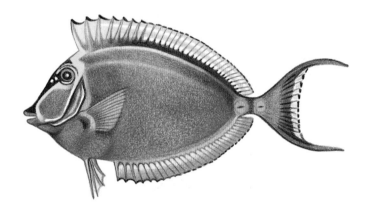

Bluespine unicornfish
Naso unicornis

Oval, tall, elongated, compressed body; forward profile marked by a beak not exceeding the mouth; pointed snout; terminal mouth with powerful compressed teeth. There are 2 bluish spines shaped like chisels and attached to bony plates on the sides of the caudal peduncle. Light gray and olive general coloring; lips sometimes blue; orange stripes on dorsal and anal fins. The caudal fin is crescent-shaped with elongated, filamentous lobes. Measures up to 24 inches (60 centimeters) long.

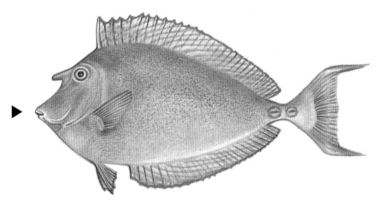

Yellowtail surgeonfish
Zebrasoma xanthurum

Body compressed laterally and covered with small scales; forward portion of the snout has typically concave silhouette; small, terminal, protractile mouth. The single dorsal fin is well developed, rounded to the rear, and almost symmetrical to the anal fin. The spines on the caudal peduncle can vary in size. Dark blue coloring with small reddish spots on the head that follow a straight line behind the eyes, ending at the pectoral fin; bright yellow caudal fin and pectoral fin edge. Measures 16 inches (40 centimeters) long.

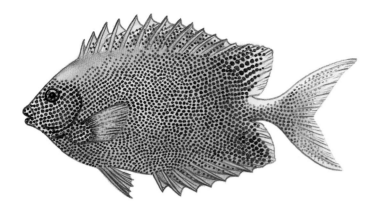

SIGANIDAE FAMILY
Stellate rabbitfish
Siganus stellatus

Oval, compressed body, covered with very small scales; slightly pointed snout; terminal mouth lined with numerous small teeth; cheeks covered with large scales. Generally grayish green coloring, spangled with small brown spots that become smaller to the back of the head, where they form a green oval shade at the base of the dorsal fin spines. Measures 16 inches (40 centimeters) long.

BLENNIIDAE FAMILY
Mimic blenny
Aspidontus taeniatus

Elongated, tapered body. Shape and coloring mimic the cleaner wrasse perfectly; even other fish have trouble distinguishing between the 2 species. The most distinctive feature of the blenny is the shape of the snout and the mouth, which turn downward due to the greater development of the upper jaw; the black band running lengthwise is also less developed. Measures up to 5 inches (13 centimeters) long.

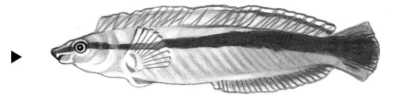

GOBIIDAE FAMILY
Sixspot goby
Valenciennea sexguttata

Tapered body covered with small, rough scales; pointed snout; mouth slightly upturned and lined with a great many teeth, some of which are quite large. Two dorsal fins: the first marked by small round or oblong blue spots. Two barely visible stripes, which do not reach the caudal fin, run along the sides. Lives part of the time buried in sandy seabeds. Measures up to 5 inches (13 centimeters) long.

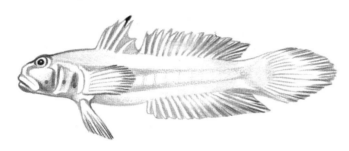

BALISTIDAE FAMILY
Orangestriped triggerfish
Balistapus undulatus

Slightly oval, tall, compressed body covered with small bony plates; very well developed head that is roughly one-third the length of the body; eyes set quite far back; terminal mouth, distinguished by powerful jaws lined with massive teeth. Background coloring is dark with contrasting orange-yellow stripes; bands of the same color surround the mouth; light blue dorsal and anal fins; yellow caudal fin. Measures up to 27 inches (70 centimeters) long.

Titan triggerfish
Balistoides viridiscens

Body shape typical of the family. Terminal mouth; deep depression between the eyes; 2 to 4 rows of large tubercles run lengthwise on the stalk of the caudal fin. Greenish coloring; fins edged in black; a black band runs around the upper jaw; stalk of the caudal fin is fairly light in color. Aggressive behavior, especially during the mating season. Measures up to 30 inches (75 centimeters) long.

Redtooth triggerfish
Odonus niger

Slightly oval body; pointed head; terminal mouth; lower jaw more developed than the upper. Body is blue-black; head is greenish with blue stripes leading from the mouth. Semilunar caudal fin, with long, well-developed lobes. Tends to gather in small groups. Measures up to 20 inches (50 centimeters) long.

Blue triggerfish
Pseudobalistes fuscus

Body shape typical of the family; rounded head; large scales under the opercula; horizontal channels along the lower portion of the snout. Dark brown coloring with yellow or orange spots on the scales; yellowish edges to the fins. Caudal fin is rounded in the young and has elongated lobes in adults. Measures up to 22 inches (55 centimeters) long.

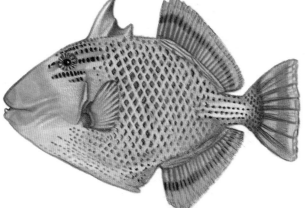

Yellowmargin triggerfish
Pseudobalistes flavimarginatus

Body shape similar to that of the blue triggerfish, but more oval. White teeth arranged in 2 rows on the upper jaw and in one row on the lower. Background coloring is fairly pale; pale yellow between the snout and the base of the pectoral fins; sides marked by numerous small black spots; edges of dorsal, anal, and caudal fins are yellowish. Measures up to 24 inches (60 centimeters) long.

Picasso triggerfish
Rhinecanthus assasi

Oval body; triangular head; pointed snout; terminal mouth. Three rows of spines on the stalk of the slightly rounded caudal fin. Yellowish lips; yellow stripe from the mouth to the operculum; a black vertical band covers the eyes; diagonal stripes on the sides. Measures up to 12 inches (30 centimeters) long.

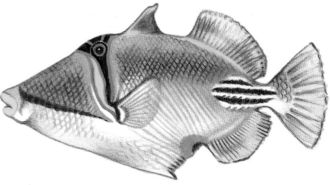

MONACANTHIDAE FAMILY
Harlequin filefish
Oxymonacanthus halli

Oval, compressed body, covered with a rough epidermis with minuscule denticles; snout typically elongated and tubular; lower jaw more developed than the upper. Green background coloring, with a regular pattern of large bright yellow or orange spots. Forms small groups near acropora branches (feeds on the polyps). Measures up to 5 inches (12 centimeters) long.

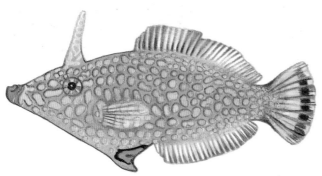

OSTRACIIDAE FAMILY
Cube boxfish
Ostracion cubicus

Rectangular body, like a box with rounded angles and corners; no spines. Small dorsal and anal fins driven by powerful muscles; ventral and caudal fins are more developed (caudal fin serves as a rudder). Males are uniformly violet; the young are yellow with black spots. Measures up to 18 inches (45 centimeters).

TETRADONTIDAE FAMILY
Blackspotted pufferfish
Arothron stellatus

Elongated, globular body with an oval silhouette, covered with small spines. The young have a rubbery texture; adults are more flaccid. Powerful mouth equipped with two large adjacent dental plates on each jaw. Coloring is typically mottled. In the young, the belly is marked by pronounced black stripes; the base of the pectoral fins is black. Propels itself with dorsal and anal fins. Commonly encountered on the sandy bottoms of lagoons. Measures up to 36 inches (90 centimeters) long.

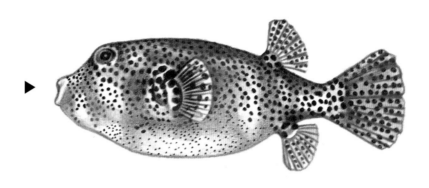

Pearl toby pufferfish
Canthigaster margaritata

Slightly compressed head and body, dotted with small spines that become clear when the fish swells. Elongated snout; protractile mouth; truncated caudal fin. At the center of the back and the belly there is a fold of skin that can erect. The dark yellow color on the back lightens on the belly; body is dotted with dark blue spots edged in black; radial stripes of the same blue surround the eyes; 2 dark blue stripes at the base of the dorsal fin. Measures up to 5 inches (13 centimeters) long.

DIODONTIDAE FAMILY
Porcupinefish
Diodon hystrix

Tapered body, rounded to the front. Large, sharp spines usually have split bases and stand erect when the fish puffs up. Mouth has a large dental plate for each jaw; snout and tail are elongated. The brownish yellow coloring is fairly dark, with numerous black spots on the sides and back. Nocturnal habits; seeks out sheltered places during the day. Divers can encounter dozens of these fish in a single dive. Measures up to 36 inches (90 centimeters) long.

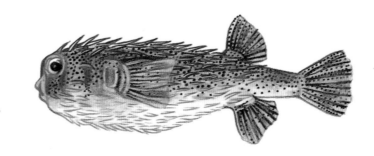

Text: Alessandro Carletti and Andrea Ghisotti
Text of "The Fish of the Red Sea":
  Angelo Mojetta
Other contributors: Massimo Bicciato, Gil
  Bunim, Claudio Cangini, Linda Chappel,
  Hanan Golombeck, Osama Rushdy
Illustrators: Cristina Franco and Arabella
  Lazzarin (dive sites); Monica Falcone
  ("The Fish of the Red Sea")

Editorial production: Valeria Manferto
  De Fabianis and Laura Accomazzo
Copyeditor: John Kinsella, Diving Science
  and Technology Corp.
Translator: Antony Shugaar
Layout: Patrizia Balocco Lovisetti
Production editor: Abigail Asher
Text designer: Barbara Sturman
Cover designer: Jennifer O'Connor

ALESSANDRO CARLETTI, a skin diving expert, was born in Milan in 1963. He has worked as a skin diving guide in the Egyptian areas of the Red Sea, both on cruise ships and at major diving centers. He is a current contributor to many Italian diving magazines.

ANDREA GHISOTTI, a specialist in underwater photography, was born in Milan in 1951. He has published more than four hundred articles about nature, the sea, diving, and photography. He has written a number of manuals on diving techniques and a book about wrecks, and has contributed to many photography books.

First edition
10 9 8 7 6 5 4 3 2 1

Library of Congress Cataloging-in-Publication Data
Ghisotti, Andrea.
  [Mar Rosso guida alle immersioni. English]
  The Red Sea dive guide / Andrea Ghisotti, Alessandro Carletti.
      p.   cm.
  Originally published: Red Sea diving guide. Shrewsbury, England : Swan Hill Press, c1994.
  Includes index.
  ISBN 0-7892-0347-2
  1. Deep diving—Red Sea—Guidebooks.   2. Scuba diving—Red Sea—Guidebooks.   3. Skin diving—Red Sea—Guidebooks.
4. Red Sea—Guidebooks.   I. Carletti, Alessandro.   II. Title.
GV838.673.R43G5513   1997
797.2'3'0916533—dc21   96-52844

Above: A coral grouper patrols the reef.
PHOTOGRAPH BY VINCENZO PAOLILLO

*Front cover:
A remarkable concentration of soft corals in a range of colors.*
PHOTOGRAPH BY PIERFRANCO DILENGE

Page 1: A group of onespot snappers lights up the water with silvery reflections.
PHOTOGRAPH BY CLAUDIO ZIRALDO

Page 2: The transparent water makes it possible to see the wall of the reef dropping away into the depths of the sea.
PHOTOGRAPH BY ANDREA GHISOTTI

Page 3: In this satellite photograph, the long strip of the Red Sea wends its way from the Sinai Peninsula to the Gulf of Aden.
PHOTOGRAPH BY WORLDSAT INTERNATIONAL

Pages 4 and 5: This photograph, taken from the space shuttle, shows the triangular shape of the Sinai Peninsula against the surface of the sea.
PHOTOGRAPH BY NASA